ALASKA

0   50   100   200   300

MILES

Map by Harry Scott

A doctor, pioneer scientist, and veteran explorer of the Arctic here tells his compassionate, firsthand story of the present-day Eskimo—and of those last few survivors, born before the arrival of the white man, who were brought up in the tradition of the ancient Stone Age hunters of the North.

Kaare Rodahl, with his wife, Joan, went to Alaska at the request of the U.S. Air Force to develop a Department of Physiology at the Arctic Aeromedical Laboratory in Fairbanks. They were to concern themselves with various scientific problems relating to man in the Arctic, and, primarily, to find out, by studying the Eskimo's adaptation to this environment, how man can become better acclimated to extreme cold.

It was an assignment that turned into a fascinating arctic adventure. It took them from the gold city of Fairbanks into the wilderness, along waterways, through endless forests, through mountain passes and across the tundra to the coast and over the ancient Eskimo trails along arctic shores and through the barrens.

For several years they worked among the Eskimo tribes and shared their daily culture.

An absorbing study of a people whose future — and fate — is uncertain, this is also a remarkable personal story, compounded of danger, hardship, humor and adventure.

THE LAST OF THE FEW

THE

LAST OF THE FEW

Kaare Rodahl, M. D.

Line drawings by Dorothy Robinson

HARPER & ROW, PUBLISHERS

New York, Evanston, and London

LIBRARY OF CONGRESS CATALOG CARD NUMBER: 63-16515

To Joan

CONTENTS

ILLUSTRATIONS

A map of Alaska follows page xii

The author is greatly indebted to Mrs. Marguerite Munson and Mr. Evan Thomas of Harper & Row for constructive advice and criticism in the preparation of the manuscript.

K.R.

1 THE ROAD TO THE NORTH

When I say that I landed by parachute in the lap of a Land Army girl in England, and married her in Oslo at the end of the war, no one believes me. And yet, truth is sometimes stranger than fiction.

Whatever the truth may be, we did meet in England during the war. It was in the spring of 1944, when Patton's armored divisions were on the move through southern England toward the Channel for the invasion. The Norwegian Parachute Company, to which I belonged, had been sent to Trowbridge to serve as guinea pigs for the pilots who were being trained to drop troops on D day. The cherry trees were in bloom, and for a paratrooper life was short and precious in those days.

This was to be my twentieth jump. I stood in the open doorway of the airplane with the parachute on my back, my left foot on the step ready to jump, my hands clutching the edge of the doorframe. Behind me stood the nineteen men waiting for the green light.

Below us, through space, we could see the ground gliding

by. We saw meadows and fields; cattle grazed in the pastures between the farm cottages. The straw roofs were partly concealed under the foliage of the oak trees. A winding footpath ran through patches of wood along a brook. Clouds passed with the wind over the sun, the shadows scurried across the field where people stood gazing into the sky as we passed.

Inside the airplane we could hear nothing but the roar of the engines. I was being pulled into the open doorway by the slip stream, my trousers were flapping in the wind, the air was howling under my helmet. I could feel the squeeze of the chin strap as I tightened my jaws to swallow.

So great was my fear now that I hardly noticed the landscape below any more. It was the jump, the dive through space and the shock of the landing, that filled my mind. I tried to think of something else, the fact that I was all set to go on leave into Trowbridge as soon as I had finished this jump. My comrades were to take my parachute back to camp for me; I was to return by bus later in the evening. If only I had this jump behind me.

And then I did not think any more. The plane tilted its nose toward the ground in a gentle descent, the engines slowed, I grasped the doorframe firmly with my hands, bent my knees as if I were trying to make myself smaller in order not to hit my head against the tail as I jumped.

There came a flash of green light. I let go, swung my right leg out, and plunged into space. It felt as if the slip stream had pulled me out by my legs. In a glance I saw the tail of the plane pass overhead as I fell on my back through the air with my hands tightly grasping the sides of my trousers. The pressure of the wind took my breath away. I felt a jigging as the strings that kept the parachute in the bag on my back were pulled apart, and heard the crackle of silk as the canopy unfolded automatically. I continued to fall. Then came a puff, as the chute suddenly opened completely, jerked violently, and I found myself being flung up in the air and turned a complete somersault. For a moment I was hanging head down, then I swung upright. I leaned back and looked up into the white silky canopy extending fully opened like a huge umbrella over me. I knew then that I was safe, at least temporarily.

As a matter of routine, I adjusted the seat straps and made myself comfortable in the harness and pulled myself up by the rigging lines a couple of times to convince myself that it all worked as it should. Then I just sat there for a few moments in ecstasy. I felt as if I were standing still in mid-air. Turning my head, I saw other parachutes suspended in a chaotic jumble in the sky. I grabbed the two forward rigging lines and pulled, and began to slide forward toward the earth.

Below I saw the field between the river and the road, surrounded by farms and forests. I could distinctly hear the voices of the people now, and could see the grass moving in the breeze. I passed a stone wall and sailed down toward a path, hanging by my arms, keeping my knees bent and legs together and my toes pointed upward as the arduous training had taught me to do.

All of a sudden the ground shot toward me. I tightened my jaws and tensed every muscle for the impact of the crash. I let go my pull on the rigging line. Instantaneously the canopy leveled off, a vertical air current caught the silk and kept it suspended in the air for a fraction of a second. Then it slowly fell toward the ground and dropped me gently in the grass. I landed standing on my feet.

I folded the parachute and carried it to the truck that was waiting on the road. Then I went into town as the sun was setting over Salisbury Plain.

I walked through the streets of Trowbridge. There were American soldiers everywhere. They filled the bars, and spent their money generously. I went to the canteen to get a meal. I ordered and took a seat in a corner. One of the volunteer workers came toward my table. She had a twinkle in her green eyes and wore a Norwegian sweater. I noticed a silver brooch on her blouse; it had the familiar picture of Arnljot Gelline on skis, carrying the baby King Haakon in his arms.

She had noticed my Norwegian uniform and wanted to know if I had recently come from Norway; did I know the little village of Kragerö among the islands in the fiord? Actually she knew as much about Norway as I did, for she had been there just before the war broke out, the year I left to go to Greenland. I gathered that she liked Norway; that she intended to go there to live as soon as the war was over.

"Joan has made up her mind to marry a Norwegian," joked the girl who brought the tea. I suggested that if this was the case I had come as a godsend, descending to her from the sky. This part of the tale was at least unquestionably true.

And this was how I happened to meet Joan. It was the ninth of April, exactly four years after the German invasion of Norway. I waited at the table until they closed the canteen for the day.

We walked through the park, she and I, and found a bench under the birches by the brook that trickled through the meadow. I was to make another jump at daybreak; meanwhile we had the whole evening before us.

Far away the tanks continued to thunder through the streets. An endless rattle of steel and armor in an interminable war. Our thoughts went far afield, as we talked, to the coast of Norway, the fiords and the string of islands to the north, to the Polar Sea and the arctic regions, where Joan hoped to go when the war came to an end.

But why to the Arctic? I asked her. Who would want to venture into the frigid North to endure a life in cold and snow and solitude when our own civilized society has so much to offer in terms of comfort, convenience and companionship?

It was not hard for me to understand, however. In my own

case, I had been captured by the fascination of the North when, at the age of twenty, I spent a year in Greenland, most of the time alone. It is an experience one never quite gets over: the complete isolation, the challenge of having to rely entirely upon oneself, the feeling of being close to undisturbed nature, the awareness of being fully alive, the thrill of exploring ground which perhaps no one else has ever walked on, to have the time in solitude to get to really know oneself, to be entirely natural and absolutely free to sleep when tired, to eat when hungry, and to work when one feels like it. And then there is the element of adventure too, the joy of anticipation, the attraction of the unknown, the yearning to venture on from one mountain crest to the next out of sheer curiosity to see what is beyond. One who has once been possessed by this spirit will never cease yearning. "Once having answered the call of the wilderness, one is always obliged to return," as the arctic explorer, Fridtjof Nansen, put it.

And so it was with Joan. She, who had been raised in London but felt at home in the peaceful fiords of Norway, sought to get away from the crowds. She wanted to experience the arctic world, see the ocean roll against the drift ice in the fog, follow the tracks of the polar bear in new-fallen snow across the floes that rise and sink with the swell; then landfall with snow-covered mountains rising from the pack ice sparkling in the midnight sun. She hoped to see smoke rise toward the frosty sky from a lonely cabin on the brink by the fiord. She wished to follow the musk ox on his wanderings through the valleys to the edge of the inland ice. She was to find her way by dog team across frozen fiords under the veils of the northern lights in the winter, and rejoice with the return of the arctic spring, when the ice breaks up in the rivers with a roar, and calving glaciers throw icebergs into the sea, and the migratory birds wing their way against the rising sun to the north.

The tanks had ceased rattling through the streets. The

brook murmured through the meadow among the white birches in the dusk. It sounded as if Joan had really made up her mind when she quoted a poem she had fancied as a child:

Let us probe the silent places, let us seek what luck betide us;
Let us journey to a lonely land I know.
There's a whisper on the night-wind, there's a star agleam to guide us,
and the Wild is calling, calling . . . let us go.

But the road which was to lead us to the north was a long and arduous one. The years passed.

We were married in 1946. I continued the study of medicine which had been interrupted by the war. At the same time we experimented with rats and vitamins in an old attic laboratory in the Institute of Physiology in Oslo, where I received my medical degree in 1948 and the Doctor of Science degree in 1950. The latter was awarded on a thesis which started with the study of the toxic effect of polar bear liver, begun during the expedition to Greenland in 1939.

Arctic travelers and explorers since the fifteenth century have known that polar bear liver is harmful to man and animals, and the Eskimos never eat it as a matter of taboo. Those who ate the liver suffered from severe headache, nausea, and a number of other symptoms, including peeling of the skin, several days after the ingestion of the liver. No one had been able to explain the reason for this ill effect.

When preparing for the Greenland expedition I decided to take up this problem for a systematic investigation. At that time I learned from my physiology professor of a legal suit resulting from the poisoning of foxes by whale liver. In the course of the court proceedings it was shown that there was nothing wrong with the whale livers sold by the whaling company to the fox farm, except that it was very rich in vitamin A, so that ingestion of this liver caused the condition known as

hypervitaminosis A in the fox. The fact that too much vitamin
A is harmful had been shown by Japanese workers some years
earlier.

It occurred to me that the cause of the toxic effect of the
polar bear liver might also simply be a matter of a high content
of vitamin A. With this in mind I undertook to collect polar
bear livers during the Greenland expedition in 1939-40. Upon
our return we analyzed the vitamin content of the bear liver
and found that it did contain huge amounts of vitamin A, and
that it would be possible to produce hypervitaminosis A if
sufficient quantities were consumed. Preliminary experiments
on rats also suggested that the toxic substance in the liver was
indeed vitamin A. Final proof would require further experiments, however. On subsequent expeditions I collected additional samples of polar bear livers, which I brought back to
the Institute of Physiology of the University of Oslo, where
Joan and I worked in a small attic laboratory next door to the
animal room. Joan, who happened to be fond of rats, had
charge of the care of the animals and of keeping the records;
I was responsible for the chemistry. Thus we toiled night and
day, seven days a week, sometimes around the clock, with no
other purpose than to prove whether or not it was the vitamin
A that was the toxic factor in the liver. In the end we were able
to show that it was.

Following the completion of this project Joan and I visited
the United States, where I served for a while in 1949 as a
special consultant in arctic nutrition to the United States Air
Force. In this connection I visited Alaska and was impressed
with the opportunities for medical research there, with the
availability of several interesting ethnic groups, a variety of
animals offering interesting physiological problems, and above
all, excellent resources for the support of field studies.

Then one day during the summer of 1950 I received a tele-
gram from Washington with an offer to go to Alaska to develop

a Department of Physiology at the Arctic Aeromedical Laboratory in Fairbanks. Joan was to go along as my laboratory technician. This was precisely what we had been waiting for.

Up to that time the Arctic Aeromedical Laboratory with a limited staff had mainly served as a field support station for visiting groups of scientists from the States. The plans now called for an expansion of this effort with the development of a full-fledged institution with a permanent staff in both basic and applied research in cold weather medicine and physiology, in line with the mission of the laboratory, which involved the study of human factors in cold weather operations.

One of the questions occupying the laboratory staff was whether man can be acclimatized to cold, so that he may be able to get along better in the Arctic. If there were such a thing as human acclimatization to cold, one would expect the Eskimos, who have been exposed to the arctic environment for generations, to be acclimatized. It would therefore be logical to start our inquiry into human acclimatization to cold with a broad study of the physiology of the Eskimo.

We would study white controls living in Fairbanks for comparison, and select representative Eskimo settlements where our main work would be concentrated. In these settlements we would establish complete field laboratories for systematic studies of the functions of the people in their natural habitat. To support these operations, the Arctic Aeromedical Laboratory had an aircraft plus crew at its disposal. We would then bring some of the Eskimos back to our laboratory for control studies under standardized conditions in our cold chamber. We would place Eskimos on white man's diet and whites on the Eskimo's diet, and see what happened.

This, then, was the beginning of our joint arctic adventure, the beginning of a mission that was to take us from the gold city of Fairbanks into the wilderness, along waterways through endless forests, through mountain passes and across the tundra to the arctic coast. There we were to take up our study of the physiology of the Eskimo, an assignment which was to take us over the ancient Eskimo trails along the arctic shores and through the barrens.

For two years we were to work among them, sharing their daily life. We were to travel and hunt with them in the remotest areas of Alaska. We were to learn about their past, their traditions, culture, customs and taboos, which would help us to predict what the future has in store for their race. We were to listen to the magic rhythm of their drum dance, take part in their whaling feasts, see the witch doctor work, learn about their myths, witness their engagement ceremonies, weddings and love life. We were to eat with them from their wooden trays on the floor, take care of their sick, deliver their babies, and help them bury their dead.

We left Norway by air one day in the fall. The weather was crisp and clear. The farmers were harvesting their fields. We landed in New York and continued on to the West Coast. The next stretch of our flight took us north from Seattle, Washington. The night was bright with full moon and northern lights. We flew in over southeastern Alaska before dawn, and on to the north over the mountains. Below us to the left we had the Pacific bathed in the moonlight, to the right a ragged coast where waves, glittering in the light, rolled into the fiords. Like shadows, the fiords cut into the landscape, from the ocean to the face of the glaciers between steep mountain slopes.

We looked down on the shadows gliding below us in the night, shadows of the archipelago where the history of Alaska began two hundred years ago. Memory of what we had heard and read about Alaska gave life to the shadows; out of the night came the picture of the past.

Russian fur traders had crossed the Ural Mountains in the sixteenth century, in 1713 they had overrun Kamchatka, and in 1741 Vitus Bering set out on his voyage on instructions from

Peter the Great. The sixty-year-old scurvy-stricken Dane made landfall over St. Elias, a mountain peak rising some 18,000 feet above the sea not far from the course we now flew. He landed on the west coast of the Kajak Island, directly below our course, and found a basket made of bark and a broken arrow by an abandoned cabin. Then Bering hoisted sails and headed for his base, which he never reached.

And now Sitka came into sight. It was here that Bering's second-in-command dropped anchor among the islands. He sent a boatload of sailors to the shore, but they failed to come back. Three days later he dispatched a second boat, but no one returned. After having waited three weeks in vain, he raised anchor and set out to sea. They never heard what happened to the landing parties, but according to an Indian myth, a chieftain dressed himself in bearskins and lured them to their death.

This was the white man's first encounter with the Tlingit tribe and this was how the history of Alaska began, a history full of bloodshed and fights against determined Indians; of suppression and massacre, and then of gold-crazy prospectors who gave their lives for the glitter of the gold dust.

Russian fur traders followed in Bering's wake. They set out from Siberia and discovered the Aleutian chain, its desolate mountains rising from the restless sea. A land of rocks and solidified lava, furrowed mountains like cones covered with bird droppings from the sea to the edge of the craters. They experienced thundering earthquakes, with a rain of fire from volcanic eruptions. In winter the wind whistled around the mountains, in summer continuous rain blanketed the hills. On the south side of the chain the sea was warm like the Japanese Current, but north of the islands the water was cold as ice.

And here they found the Aleuts, a group of Eskimos who called themselves the "Brothers of the Sea Otter." They were short of stature but sturdily built; they had sparse hair growth and the color of their skin was like that of the people of northern Japan. The sea was their environment. In their skin-covered bidarkas they paddled through the breakers with their bows and arrows and primitive tackle on hunting and fishing expeditions. They were a peaceful Stone Age people, and so they were conquered and partly exterminated. Now there are less than four thousand of them left.

The Russian fur traders from Siberia pushed on to the east. They found that the islands became larger as they continued eastward with hills covered with grass and lava rising from the sea into foothills farther inland, where glaciers bridged the fiords. This was the vast territory of the Tlingit Indians, a proud, courageous and ruthless tribe living in a highly organized society. They lived in large log cabins, many families together in one room. Like the Vikings, they traveled great distances in their long boats on plundering expeditions looking for slaves. Each boat carried as many as twenty warriors, equipped with helmet, cuirass and shield. There are now only a few thousand left of this tribe, and about as many Athapascan Indians in the interior of Alaska.

As we passed overhead in the plane we saw the lights of Sitka in the night. On the hill above the harbor Baranov, manager of the Russian-American Company, had built his wooden castle in 1802, ruled ruthlessly over the Aleuts and fought against the Indians. At that time it was a glamorous and gay city with spectacular balls and colorful costumes. The adventurers, warriors and fur traders all congregated there. And it was in Sitka, the old capital, that the Americans first hoisted the flag when they bought Alaska from the Russians on October 18, 1867.

The day dawned as we approached the Alaska Range at an altitude of 10,000 feet. New snow covered the peaks, glowing in the rays of the rising sun. To the north as far as one could see across the plains between the Alaska Range and the Endicott Mountains, lakes and rivers twinkled in the sun. In the hills we saw the scars of forest fires, burned-out wasteland, rust-colored logs, and underbrush growing up from the ashes.

"How vast it is!" said Joan, who was visibly overwhelmed and recalled that the word "Alaska" had something to do with vastness.

Approaching Alaska this way from the sky one is impressed with the appropriateness of the name which actually means "The Great Land." It covers an area larger than Scandinavia. It reaches from the mild, moist Pacific Sector in the south to the arctic coast in the north, the hunting ground of the 15,000 Eskimo population of Alaska.

It is also a land of great contrasts. Endless stretches of un-inhabited tundra separate modern cities; strawberries ripen at the foot of the glaciers and vegetables grow close to the edge of active volcanoes. In the sea off the Alaskan coast one may catch anything from shrimps to whales. Alaska's resources include salmon, gold, coal and fur; in the interior there are vast areas of forest and land suitable for cultivation. The summer temperature may approach 100° F., in winter it may drop to 60° below zero.

In the exact geographical center of this huge country is Fairbanks, "Alaska's Golden Heart." The town was founded as a prospector's camp at the banks of the Chena River, when Felix Pedro struck gold in the Pedro Creek in 1902. It developed into a small community of a couple of thousand settlers who enjoyed a peaceful and comfortable existence until World War II. With the war came the establishment of Ladd Field at the outskirts of the town, where Russian pilots collected the planes that the Americans turned over to them under the Lend-Lease agreement.

Today Fairbanks is a busy pioneer town with a population of about 20,000 who look optimistically to the future. It is one of the main centers for the extensive gold mining that is still one of the important industries in Alaska. Here is also one of the state's two universities, a few miles outside the city. Once more Fairbanks has become a center of considerable military significance; there is enormous construction activity and much talk of oil, gas, coal, uranium, lumber and hydroelectric power.

This is where the railroads from the coast come to an end, the Alcan Highway from Canada terminates here, and this is where the long-distance airplanes from the outside world come down. This is where the more primitive methods of transportation into the wilderness begin, by bush plane and dog team.

Here one will still find the old one-story log cabins behind pavements of cement. These crumbling, lop-sided shacks of bark-covered logs, with peat-covered roofs, serve as a reminder of the colorful past when the saloon girls danced for a fee in gold dust on 4th Street. Now skyscrapers rise twelve stories above these cabins. Hotels, restaurants and bars have replaced the saloons, but the stores still remain where for a whole generation the trappers fitted out in the fall for their lonely existence in the wilderness, and the prospectors equipped for their expeditions during the brief arctic summer.

There are few places in the world where the airplane has played such an important role as in Alaska. Huge mountain ranges, impregnable forests and endless tundra separate the settlements, and often there are many miles between settlers. Not long ago it took weeks by dog team to travel from one cabin to another in the winter, or by canoe along the waterways in the summer. Today regularly scheduled air routes connect outposts with the towns. Trappers fly to their cabins in the wilderness, and mail and provisions may be dropped by plane in front of their doors. Even before the war Alaskan airlines carried twenty-three times as many passengers and a thousand times as much cargo per inhabitant as the United States lines, and this trend continues. The important air routes to the Far

East already pass over Alaska. Almost daily commercial airlines cross the North Pole from Scandinavia to Alaska and continue on to Tokyo. The large airfields in Alaska are important bases in global strategy.

The airliner that brought us to Alaska let down over Fairbanks and landed at Ladd Field early in the morning of September 8. We drove to the Arctic Aeromedical Laboratory with a suitcase full of projects. We ourselves were filled with enthusiasm and impatient to get started.

2 AKIVIAK

Finally, in the middle of November, we were ready for the expedition to Kaktovik, where our venture was to begin.

We had elected to start with this tiny Eskimo settlement on the north coast of Alaska for several reasons: first of all, a small air base nearby made it easily accessible and, second, it was a well-defined settlement controlled by its chief, Akiviak, who was known as an outstanding individual whose co-operation we could count on.

According to the anthropologists, the Eskimos, who belong to the Mongoloid stock, probably came from Asia by way of Bering Strait some two thousand to three thousand years ago. They continued eastward along the rim of the Polar Sea as far as the east coast of Greenland. Some of them branched off into the interior, into the tundra and northern mountain ranges of Alaska and Canada, where they roamed most of the year as nomadic caribou hunters. These were the inland Eskimos, or Nunamiuts, of whom there are now only the Anaktuvuk Pass Eskimos and Canadian Caribou Eskimos left. While the world's

15

50,000 Eskimos are similar in appearance and physical features, and speak the same basic language, they may differ to some extent in diet, clothing, and living habits, depending upon the location and type of game and fur animals available. These differences were taken into account when we selected the Eskimo settlements for our studies.

For many weeks we had labored with our preparations, checking and trying out every item of equipment, for out on the coast we would have no one but ourselves to rely on and no opportunity for repair or replacement. Meticulously, Joan prepared detailed lists of every item of equipment as it was packed in labeled boxes. She spent most of her time bending over the packing cases amidst piles of supplies on the floor of the old warehouse that served as our laboratory in those days before the new laboratory building was completed. Occasionally the heat went off or the steampipes froze, and we had to haul in a Herman Nilson heater of the type used for heating airplane engines on the flight line, to blow hot air into the laboratory to prevent our reagents from freezing.

In one corner a brilliant, young, shortsighted and absent-minded biologist was searching for ticks in an anesthetized porcupine. A husky and eager physiologist was working on a huge bear in a hibernating cage underground. His problem was to measure the rectal temperature of the bear with a set of thermocouples during hibernation. One day the scientist came galloping out of the cage chased by the bear, which had taken hold of the thermocouples, and it looked for a moment as if the two had reversed their roles.

A young zoologist was trying to find out why the snow buntings did not freeze their feet when standing on the snow crust which at times was as cold as $-60°$ F. From dusk to dawn he crawled around in the woods and seemed to suffer more than the birds. Then at last one day he came barging into the laboratory with rime frost in his beard to announce that

the dispensary at our disposal for a laboratory and
rs for Joan and myself; the neighboring Jamesway was
se our X-ray equipment and would serve as quarters for
o technicians. Finally a heated tent was to be used for
etabolism studies.

air base was manned by men only. At that time women
uled out at any of the air bases north of Brooks Range.
vas the first to be allowed into this isolated outpost. A
er of people had wondered what would happen, but it
d out far better than anyone had predicted. The men
showed her every courtesy and consideration, and they
repared for her arrival in the most thoughtful manner.
.octor had arranged for the manufacture of a folding
 which was to be placed around her bed as a shield,
very hour, on the hour, all night long, a guard was to
r with a flashlight to check the stove for her safety and
rt. The sergeant had loaded his pistol and insisted that
vas to keep it under her pillow, just in case. It remained
 the pillow untouched as long as we stayed there, but
onally she would dream about the dangerous weapon
 she undoubtedly feared more than any possible intruder.
other, and more delicate, problem was the fact that there
nly one latrine in the entire camp, a shack with ten seats
e bank by the Polar Sea, commonly known as the "throne
 of ten seats." A red-hot oil stove in the middle of the
heated the place, a lonely light bulb was tied to a pole
le the door, more for navigational purposes than anything
The medic who served as our official host arranged that
time Joan needed to avail herself of this facility I was
rform a proper reconnaissance and then remain standing
e pole as a guard to inform those who might appear that
nack was engaged. This turned out to be an uncomfortable
ment in the stormy winter nights when the wind was so
g that it raised the lids of the seats, and I was on my

he had discovered the trick. He had actually observed how the
snow bunting occasionally pressed its tail and wing tips against
the snow surface, supporting itself on these three points while
lifting its feet off the ground to warm them against its chest.

In the middle of all this the base commander announced
that he would be coming around on an inspection. The GIs were
so busy dusting the corners that they failed to notice the general
as he came through. The only one who saw him was Joan, who
almost ran him down in the hallway as she came bouncing along
with an armful of toilet rolls. "I beg your pardon," said she.
"As you were," said the general, and had no further comments.

At that time Ladd Field was a small place; everything was
within shouting distance, and everyone knew everyone else
by his first name. For several months, between field trips,
Joan and I lived in a small room in the Bachelor Officers
Quarters and ate in the Officers Club. The BOQ was noisy, and
like so many of these military buildings, hurriedly put together,
it was overheated and there was no way of regulating the
radiators, which used to keep us awake at night by bursts of
explosionlike noises, banging and hissing of steam. More than
once we were awakened to find an officer standing in the middle
of the floor with his bags, saying, "Sorry, it must be the wrong
room," as indeed it was.

As our preparations went forward, our faithful and good-
natured pilot, Jim Hammer, would poke his nose into the laboratory. With a big grin he would shake his head as the heap of
equipment mounted, mumbling something to the effect that it
was already too much for one load; we would never get off the
ground with all that. Joan had only to remind him that he
had claimed that as long as we could physically shove it into
his blessed C-47 he could guarantee that the Ole Goony Bird
could take off.

At last, four tons of equipment and supplies were carefully
packed in numbered boxes, enough to set up a complete labora-

tory at the coast with all that it entailed—instruments for medical examinations, including a portable X-ray machine and a gadget for testing night vision, syringes for taking blood samples, reagents, test tubes, water bath, balances, and instruments for analysis of blood and urine, spirometers to measure basal metabolism, scales to weigh the Eskimos' food, calipers for anthropometric measurements, folding tables, cots and chairs, and a portable generator to produce our own electrical power.

Now we were all set, the schedule worked out in every detail. A brand-new flying boxcar, which was being test-flown for the first time in the Arctic, was ready to take us north to the coast.

The day was sunny, the temperature was 30° below. From the crack of dawn we scurried around, excited and confused, to take care of the various last-minute details. Trucks loaded with equipment were backed up to the plane, the huge door at the back was opened, and the load was pulled straight into the aircraft while heaters blew hot air into the fuselage to prevent the chemicals from freezing. When the crew chief was asked if they could put on, in addition, a couple of tons of fuel oil and provisions, two hundred cases of beer for the air base on the coast, he agreed to take the beer, but preferred to forget about the oil.

Then came the passengers: Sergeant Jim Edwards and Corporal Bob Blakely, who served as our faithful and loyal laboratory technicians, and finally the two of us.

After the usual fuss and apparent confusion which always seems to be normal routine in the eyes of a passenger in a bucket seat in the rear end of a military plane, we became airborne and started to climb. We gained altitude very slowly, almost touched the treetops as we flew across the hills toward the Yukon River. For a while we wondered whether we would be able to climb across Brooks Range, but eventually we could feel in our ears that we were gaining altitude. We crossed the range above the fog at 12,500 feet.

North of the range the clouds broke at last, unfold[ing a] rugged snow-covered landscape. Rivers and valleys cut [their] way through the mountains, with steep precipices and [jagged] peaks on either side, rivers wound through valleys [that] opened into grass-covered spaces farther to the north. B[elow] us the jagged peaks of the lifeless Endicott Mounta[ins ap]peared in endless succession, until they vanished behind [as] the northern slopes stretched down from the foothill[s to the] Polar Sea.

The sun had set and it was already twilight when w[e reached] the northern foothills and flew out over the slope to[ward the] coast. Scattered herds of caribou grazed on the tu[ndra, un]doubtedly the forerunners of the great herds that w[ould] be following across the barrens.

Away in the distance we could distinguish the [sea] stretching northward to eternity. We were told to [fasten our] seat belts, and then we started to descend. As we [sank we] caught a glimpse of the Polar Sea, waves break[ing on] floating ice. Then the Eskimo village of Kaktov[ik came in] sight.

Our plane touched down on a strip of icy gra[vel] across the sandspit of an island close to the main[land,] the site of an ancient Eskimo village long si[nce gone. The] present village of Kaktovik is farther to the wes[t.] It was made up of half a dozen huts of driftw[ood,] cardboard and sod, built over permafrost upon [the] sea. The nearby Air Force installation consiste[d] of Jamesway huts on either side of a snow-co[vered road.]

The night was clear and cold, as we landed [and wind] swept the snow across the lagoon; beyond it [gleamed] lights from the camp.

A couple of tracked over-snow vehicles [came to the] door of the plane, a crew of eager airmen h[elped unload] our boxes and to transport all our equipmen[t]

knees outside, hanging onto the light pole to avoid being swept into the sea.

As soon as we had unpacked our equipment and checked our instruments we were ready to start our studies. So we set out for the Eskimo village to arrange for the subjects.

The medic served as our main contact, so he led the way. The rest of us followed him across the crusty snow toward the settlement, a few hundred yards from the camp. He was well informed and briefed us as we walked. There upon the hill was the graveyard; from the middle of it protruded the tail of an airplane that had crashed. The empty oil drums filled from the "throne room of ten seats" were out on the ice to our right. They would drift with the ice toward Siberia at breakup, he explained.

Behind the medic came Joan, enthusiastic and gay, wearing slippery caribou mukluks and a blue flying suit with the hood pulled over a woolen cap so that only her nose was visible in the opening. Then came the corporal, pleasant and polite, with crooked knees and a drop hanging from his nose. The sergeant was round and placid, although quite meticulous and stubborn at times, but very likable when he smiled and showed the missing tooth in the front of his upper jaw. Both sergeant and corporal were trained laboratory technicians. I came last, knock-kneed and heavy, stamping through the snow with a frozen cigar stump in my mouth. Thus the scientists approached the people of the Stone Age.

The chief's hut was the largest and closest to the camp; at the top of the bank it overlooked the rest of the dwellings. From this position he ruled over his people and his congregation of twenty-six souls with firmness and kindness. "He is their minister too," explained the medic. "They all depend on him; his word is law here."

The village lay exposed to wind and weather. A westerly storm swept across the tundra between the mountains and the sea, sweeping the snow across the unsheltered barrens. The landfast ice was cracking under the pressure of the tide. Faint lights twinkled from the small windows of the sod-covered huts ahead of us. The trail of the northern lights flickered under a dark sky above.

As we entered the house through the narrow hallway we stumbled over a washtub in a corner filled with urine used for tanning hides. We opened a door and looked into a room where a half dozen Eskimos were squatting in a circle on the floor around a tray filled with boiled caribou meat and frozen fish. Some of them were pulling the skin off the fish with a knife, cutting the flesh from the bones with their teeth. Others were eating strips of caribou meat, which they sliced in suitable pieces with a knife held in front of their lips. They smiled and got up as we entered, licking the fat from their fingers.

By the wall sat a very old woman with blue tattoos on her chin: three parallel lines from the lower lip produced by sinew and soot soaked in urine. A young boy stood in a corner and played with an accordion. In a bed by the door lay a baby asleep.

The walls were covered with the pages of a mail-order catalogue, and the room was brightly lit by electricity produced by their own generator which rattled in a shed nearby.

In the background by the window facing the sea stood Akiviak, the chieftain, watching the children. He was in his sixties, but looked younger. He was not tall, by white man's standards, but he was slender, agile, erect, and had a keen and vital appearance. His costume was colorful—a bright yellow shirt over blue slacks and a pair of caribou mukluks with red, black and white trimmings of imported calfskin. His skin was smooth and thin and almost free of fat so that his veins were clearly visible. Thin black hair covered part of his high forehead; his nose was large and curved. His dark eyes, under the bushy eyebrows, searched us with intense curiosity.

"Sjumitutin!" he shouted in a hoarse voice as a welcome. He had a habit of shouting, for he was hard of hearing. Then he smiled at us, as only Eskimos can smile. One of his front teeth was so loose that it wiggled when he spoke. Apparently all the rest of his teeth were intact but the chewing of dried or frozen meat during a lifetime had worn them down to the gums.

We explained the purpose of our visit and requested his co-operation in the study of his people. In return we would offer medical care and any other service that they might need. Without hesitation he granted our request, and thus began a friendship for life.

He was the minister and the master, the head of the people of Kaktovik, and his decisions were final. He was well read and well informed. When he spoke he used a language that was almost lyrical, and in his features there was nothing to betray that he, as a boy, had been a primitive hunter of the north, on endless migration along the waterways from the mountains to the shores of the Polar Sea with the bow and arrow as his weapon. Bit by bit, while we were there, he told us the story of his life in the simple words of a man who had seen the culture of a Stone Age change to Atomic Age civilization within the space of his lifetime.

His tribe, "the people of the land," or Nunamiuts, had come from the west, from the region of the Utukok River between Wainwright and Point Lay. He was born in a tent on the bank of the river at the time of the freeze-up in the year 1889. At that time his tribe was still untouched by civilization. In his childhood he knew of no village; to him no land or life existed beyond the fringe of the frozen sea in the west and north and the high-peaked, snow-covered mountains to the east and south. His world was one of hills and tundra, and rivers down to the coast, for his people were nomadic tribes constantly on the move in seasonal migration along the waterways between the mountains and the sea. They paddled in their skin boats, the umiaks, on the river in the summer and raced by dog sledge over the frozen tundra in the fall. They followed the caribou trail like the wolves and, like the wolves, their life was one of feast and famine.

Among his earliest recollections was the endless convoy of skin boats that late in the summer moved up the river toward the foothills of the mountains. Five dogs towed each boat along the bank by ropes made of walrus skin. When the ice formed on the river in the fall they put up their boats on the bank where they had left the sledges in the spring.

Here the families gathered and built their tents of caribou skins stretched over willow, with a skylight made of the dried intestine of bearded seal. A bearskin covered the door. The women kindled the fire with flint and moss within a ring of rocks in the center of the tent where they cooked the meat.

In the long autumn evenings Akiviak listened to his father's tales of the tundra until he went to sleep between layers of deerskin spread over a mat of willow and sage. In the daytime he would sit silent on a hillcrest for hours, watching the men make knives, spearheads, arrowheads and scrapers from flint they had collected along the Utukok River.

Then came days of famine when the caribou failed. They lashed their belongings onto the sledges and moved on across the barrens. Every day at the end of the trail they would build an igloo of deerskins and willow. In the morning they would rise before daybreak to eat a slice of meat with a small amount of melted snow before they started on the journey. When the snow was deep his father would harness himself to the sledge, while his mother drove the dogs.

Those were the hungry days. But with the coming of spring the caribou herds returned from the south, flowing like a living river out over the barrens. The Nunamiuts manned the corrals and the runners drove the herd into a funnel lined with willow bundles shaped like men, placed in a double row, converging toward the corral where the bewildered deer were caught in the snares or stabbed or killed by flint-headed arrows.

Late in the spring they drove their sledges to the river again. Here, at the time of the breakup, they left them on the bank and drifted down the stream in their umiaks to trade their skins and caribou meat for blubber and maktaq with the Eskimos on the coast. And every summer, year after year, Eskimos from Point Hope came to meet them at the mouth of the Utukok River to trade and to dance.

Relations between the tribes were not always so friendly. He could remember hostilities between the Nunamiuts and the people of the coast, when men disappeared and bows and arrows were constantly carried in readiness for protection against the intruders.

He was a boy, "so small that the tail of a ptarmigan tied to his belt by its head would reach to the ground," when the rifle was first used by his people. It belonged to his cousin who had got it in trade for a dog from an Eskimo on the coast. He remembered seeing his cousin kill a ptarmigan with it, but the old people refused to eat the bird which had been killed with the gun.

He was five years old when the game disappeared and starvation forced the Nunamiuts to leave the mountains. Then began his life among the people of the coast in endless wandering along the shores of the Arctic Ocean, living in skin tents in the summer and building igloos of driftwood and sod for the winter.

He learned how to hunt ducks with a sling, to harpoon walrus in the water, and to catch seal with a net along open leads in the ice. And while the ice was still in the bay he went out with the men in the skin boats to kill whales.

It was then that he first met the white man. A large boat with sails came in from the sea; it had white men on board who were traders. From then on they traded regularly with the passing whalers every summer, receiving molasses and flour in return for their baleen.

At the age of eleven Akiviak lost his father; and his grandfather took the family to Oktiavik, a village by the Arctic Ocean. This was in the year 1900.

The eleven-year-old boy walked into the village bewildered, for he could hardly believe what he saw: large wooden houses with windows of glass, a church, a schoolhouse, and a store full of things that he had never seen or heard of before. Crowds of people moved about between the houses; others lived in tents on the sandspit. He met children who said they went to school, where they learned how to pray and to write the language of the whites.

Soon after they arrived his mother died, and the children were left as strangers in the village. Some of the people gave them food and asked them to stay, but others were superstitious and wanted no strangers to come to their igloo, for it meant bad luck according to the shaman. So, many times they had to sit outside in the storm to eat the frozen meat with their bare hands.

It was then that Akiviak began to go to school and learn how to read and to write. But when the whaling season started in May even the young boys had to go out with the men on the ice for the hunt. The twelve-year-old Akiviak became one of the crew, and many whales were killed that year.

While half the crew kept watch the other half slept in their clothes on the ice. When a whale was sighted, they all manned the skin boats and paddled cautiously toward it. Once close enough, the striker in the bow of the boat would sink his harpoon deep into the muscles of the whale. Several seal floats* attached to the harpoon head by walrus rope hampered the whale in its attempts to dive, until it was so exhausted and

---

* The dried skin of a seal made into an airtight bag which is blown up with air into a balloon.

weak that it could be killed by the spears. Then a flag was hoisted on the mast as a signal for the other whaleboats to come help tow the whale to the shore ice, where it was butchered.

When the fleet of skin boats returned to the village at the end of the season the success of the whale hunt was celebrated with a feast and blanket tossing, as had been the custom of these people from the earliest times. The large walrus-skin blanket, held by the strongest of the men, could toss a person twenty-five feet into the air, and occasionally someone failed to land on the blanket and broke a leg or an arm, but the crowd cheered and laughed and had a wonderful time. Then followed the drum dance in which the various whaling crews were joined by their wives. While they danced, gifts were tossed to the elders, according to tradition.

The following summer the "great sickness" came upon the people. Akiviak saw them die in the skin boats while traveling along the coast. Those that survived struggled on by foot across the tundra, living on sea gulls, owls and some foxes. As they staggered into the village they found whole families dying from an illness—the flu—that they had never seen before.

In the years that followed, he observed the steadily increasing influence of the white man on Eskimo life. He saw schooners arriving with white man's food and trading goods; he saw white man's ships crushed in the ice, the marooned crews eventually reaching the village. Hired as an interpreter for a trader, he traveled along the coast from settlement to settlement. The trader would invite the Eskimos on board the ship, and before the natives had a chance to transfer to their umiaks the supplies for which they had bartered he would start the engine and move away.

"But Eskimos never forget," said Akiviak. "White man put things in his notebook to remember. The Eskimo never writes, but still he remembers all that is promised to him."

Akiviak married at the age of twenty-one. Four years later he became a Sunday-school teacher, and in 1915 was hired as a seaman on board a ship bound for Herschel Island in the Canadian Arctic. Here he met Eskimos who spoke a dialect different from his own and went to church on Sunday and sang hymns translated into the Eskimo language.

In 1916 he moved with his family to the east, attracted by the abundance of game he had seen the previous year during his voyage to Herschel. He settled at Demarkation Point. In the fall he hunted sheep in the mountains and caribou on the tundra, and in the spring he caught seal with seal nets under the ice while the women hooked tomcods in the lagoon.

In the fall of 1921 he came to Kaktovik, where he built his house of driftwood and sod at the site of the ancient village on the sandspit. Then followed a prosperous time, for there was an abundance of game, and in some years he made over $2,000 in fox skins.

By 1926 he owned a large herd of reindeer and a motor launch with a 20-horsepower engine. In 1933 he was elected ruling elder of the Presbyterian Church and later became the Presbyterian minister. He became the governing chief of the Eskimo group that gathered around him at Kaktovik on the shore of the Polar Sea.

And so his life went on through changing periods of feast and famine until 1947, when the white man moved in and built an air strip near the site of his village. This marked the beginning of the final stage of the invasion of the white man's culture.

From year to year the Eskimo's habits changed with the irreversible process of civilization. White man's garments took the place of his clothing of fur; bread and butter, hot cakes and candy largely replaced his ancient diet of blubber and meat. Movies took the place of the telling of tales handed down from father to son through generations.

But throughout the years of drastic change Akiviak preserved the best from his own upbringing, pride in the traditions of his people flavored with the best from the white man's teaching. Yet deep in his soul the spirit of the ancient Eskimo still remained.

It was late one evening when Akiviak came to the end of his story. He had been sitting on the bed by the window, pausing occasionally to listen to the gale shaking the house.

On the floor in front of the fire two of his sons were working on the drums. The dried walrus stomachs, which had been soaked in a bucket of water, were stretched over frames of willow boughs with a handle of driftwood, and tied to the frame with caribou sinew.

Akiviak had six sons and three daughters living. He had had many more children but they died at birth or shortly thereafter. His wife had died of cancer a few years before and was buried up on the hill.

"Now I am lonely and cold in my bed," said Akiviak. He was looking thoughtfully out the window; then his eyes fell on lovely Rebecca, a bashful, well-developed teen-ager, standing by the wall. As he viewed her with apparent affection, she blushed and looked down.

"I intend to marry Rebecca—she has promised to marry me." Four times she had promised to wed him and three times changed her mind. And so we learned that Eskimos have their problems too, in spite of their smiles and happy appearance.

"Rebecca is poor," reasoned Akiviak, "she has to work very hard, and must go hungry to bed. In the morning she goes to school without breakfast."

Akiviak had offered her food at his table; he was generous and presented her with precious gifts, for he needed her affection. "My heart is with her," he said, "and she has said that she loves me."

Akiviak was lonely; he still had the urge, and he had tempted her with money, $2,000 in the bank. He offered security, prestige, respect and a honeymoon to Fairbanks. Finally she made up her mind; the advantages were too obvious to refuse. Now Akiviak was bubbling over and delighted to find someone like us to share all this with. We listened in silence and wished him well.

Throughout the evening of our first call on Akiviak the Eskimos kept coming in, individually or in families, banging the snow off their mukluks, smiling and disappearing through the door into the "schoolhouse." We now joined them there, and after a short Bible reading Akiviak looked at his watch, cleaned his glasses with a rag, took up his Bible and joined his congregation in the schoolhouse.

Akiviak briefed them on our studies. Earlier in the evening we had prepared a list of subjects with their individual appointments for the different tests and instructions on how to behave and what to do.

For practical reasons, we had elected to start with those tests which were painless to create confidence and reduce apprehension. The next morning, therefore, we began an X-ray examination of the entire village.

It all went smoothly. Smiling and joking, they appeared punctually and showed the greatest interest in our progress. Indeed, they participated with such intelligence that it was a joy to work among them, and they proved to be better and more reliable subjects than many of our whites.

Akiviak was the first to be examined in order to give the others confidence. But he insisted on an X ray of his head so that he could see what he looked like inside. He had suffered from headaches for a good many years, ever since he once, as a young man, fell in the mountains while hunting sheep. We granted his request but found nothing visibly wrong, and gave him the picture as a present. But this was a mistake, for soon

every Tom, Dick and Harry complained of headaches and requested X rays of their heads.

The corporal was in charge of the X rays. He measured and
exposed and maneuvered the Eskimos about until the heavy
X-ray machine almost went through the flimsy wooden floor
of the Jamesway.

The Eskimos would come to the dispensary one at a time,
Akiviak serving with obvious pleasure as the interpreter. We
started with a thorough history of each subject, followed by a
detailed physical examination from head to foot. We were
particularly interested in finding out whether or not these
primitive people suffered from the so-called diseases of civilization, such as atherosclerosis, high blood pressure and peptic
ulcer. We did find, as expected, that tuberculosis was probably
the most serious medical problem, otherwise they appeared to
suffer from the same kinds of complaints which one sees among
any white group, and in many ways the medical picture reminded me to a great extent of what I had seen among the
isolated fishing villages in northern Norway. There was one
striking difference, however—their blood pressure was defi-
nitely lower and peptic ulcers appeared to be unknown. Con-
trary to expectations, hardening of the arteries was not at all
uncommon. While the old Eskimos were completely free of
dental caries, the dental condition of the children was ap-
palling.

From a series of blood tests we found that their hemoglobin
was generally quite low, so that mild anemia was a frequent
condition. Their sedimentation rate—the rate with which the
red blood cells settle to the bottom of a test tube containing
freshly drawn blood—was often high, which is a common finding in many types of infection. In their urine we were surprised
to find no trace of ketone bodies, although they lived on a
ketogenic diet. It is generally assumed that the Eskimo's diet
is very high in fat. This we found not to be the case; in fact,

the percentage of calories furnished from fat was no higher than that of our white controls. The protein intake, on the other hand, was far greater than ours, on account of their high meat consumption.

Their basal metabolism we found to be high, as had been reported earlier, but some of this was due to the state of anxiety on the part of the patients who were unaccustomed to such tests, for as we repeated the test on successive days we observed a significant reduction in the basal metabolism. But still their basal metabolic rate was significantly higher than normal, and this had to be looked into further.

In the evenings we carried on a regular clinic activity and treated their various illnesses, among which constipation was by far the most common. Joan helped the mothers off and on with their long colorful parkas, and pulled the babies out from under their mothers' hoods. She took a special interest in the children, and bandaged their many wounds and treated their sore fingers.

Akiviak watched with a smile and wanted to know about everything. In the evening when the rest of them had gone he remained behind and sat by the hour telling about his life.

Sometimes at night the storm blew the door to the laboratory open, and the snow piled high on the floor, so that we had to shovel our way to the test tubes. In the mornings we fought our way to the Eskimo village to survey their diet and to weigh what they ate. We stamped through the snow against the storm from one dwelling to another, watched the women frying pancakes, which they served with syrup followed by porridge with sugar and canned milk, then bread with peanut butter and, finally, coffee or tea. The little children crawled around among packing cases on the earth floor, eating with their fingers and washing their hands after, instead of before, the meal.

One evening the entire village gathered in the room used as a classroom in the daytime and a church in the evenings and on Sundays. They shook the snowflakes off their cotton-covered parkas as they entered, and sat quietly down by the wall.

Three of the men placed themselves cross-legged on the floor in the middle of the room, each of them holding a drum by the handle. For a while the drummers fiddled with the drums while the audience argued as to what songs they should sing.

Slowly the drummers began to mumble, then came some kind of humming song. The voices rose and sank rhythmically with occasional shouts: auu, yah iah, the drumsticks hit the frame of the drum with a bang. The drummers tightened their fists around the sticks so that their knuckles whitened. The song rose and fell, the shouts became louder, the crowd in the background, which had gradually become absorbed by the mysticism of the song and the rhythm, joined in the refrain: unghi-yah, angha-yah, yah yah yah . . .

Suddenly a fourteen-year-old hunter named Apayaok sprang forward onto the dance floor to perform the dance of the caribou hunt. He shuffled and quivered, bending his knees and tramping the floor, waving his arms and twisting his head with the rhythm of the drums.

This was a solo performance. Then came the pair dance, when a woman and a man danced together in their fur boots and parkas, galloping on the floor without moving so much as a yard. They sang about the whale hunt and the fool who refused to dance.

The tempo increased, the songs became louder, while more and more of the crowd joined in the chant. Soon there was no pause between songs. The dancers came forward without halt or hesitation. The drummers hit the drums like madmen, their eyes tightly closed and their faces soaked with sweat, swaying forth and back with the rhythm of the song.

They sang of the great hunters of the north, of the whales

and bears and seals and the caribou, with the self-derision and the peculiar sense of humor characteristic of these people, but obscure to the stranger.

The monotony of the drums became fascinating, the spirit of the songs contagious. The Eskimos became once again the primitive people by the spirit of the unwritten songs of their ancestors handed down from father to son through generations from the earliest times.

An old lady, Putugook, had been watching the dance from a corner in the rear of the crowd, her head tilted to one side, her lips slightly vibrating. As the excitement rose she seemed increasingly moved. She began to wave her arms and to shake her body. Suddenly she leapt forward and joined the dancers on the floor. She danced with such vigor it was hard to believe that she was a woman in the eighties and almost crippled with arthritis.

Then the chief himself, Akiviak, danced a solo. He posed like a statue, his muscles were tense like a steel spring. His right foot moved forward; he bent his knee, stepping on the floor with his heel in keeping with the rhythm of the drums. He raised one arm, stretched the other toward the floor, twisted it and made a move as if he pointed at the deer, bending his body as if he was to sneak in on the prey. Then a final bang of the drums, which sounded like a gunshot, brought the dance to an end.

Two little girls, about three years old, appeared on the floor. They stood with their big wondering eyes gazing ahead, waving their arms and twisting their bodies to the rhythm of the drums. All of a sudden one of them became quiet; she ceased to move. A puddle appeared where she stood, it poured in a stream across the floor toward the place where one of the drummers was sitting. A woman bent down and began to mop with a sock. Then the drummer opened his eyes, looked at the puddle for a moment, moved to one side, closed his eyes again, and continued to hammer on his drum.

And so the dance went on through the night: ung hiyah, ah ha yah . . .

In the morning a copper-colored line rose in the horizon over the pack ice in the east, where the first dawn of day would soon appear. There was a breeze of cold air from the Arctic Ocean, where hummocks and pack ice glimmered in a hazy mirage in the twilight. The only sound was the thunder from the ice as it yielded and cracked under the pressure of the sea.

I was standing outside the laboratory listening, for I expected there might be bears around in such weather. And I was waiting to see the ptarmigan which had spent the night in the hollows by the landbrink take to their wings to return to the mountains for the day.

Then I heard the crushing and ringing sound of footsteps on the frozen snow crust; they came from the Eskimo village, rapid steps across the hill toward the ice. It was Akiviak setting out to hunt. He moved like a youth across the tundra, bouncing and agile, bowlegged, his small feet moving in short, rapid steps. He wore caribou mukluks, white snow parka and trousers. The rifle was hanging on his back in a skin bag.

He had been out of bed before 5 A.M., dressed in darkness, and set out without breakfast. "The best hunter is the man who is first out," he would say, "for he may get to the game before anyone else has had a chance to scare it away."

As a rule, he sneaked out alone while the rest of the village was still asleep, to look for polar bears on the ice. Later his sons would follow with their dog teams, carrying on the sledge a primus stove, some tea or coffee, bread, sugar and frozen or boiled meat. In addition they took sleeping bags, a small tent, and some extra kerosene for the primus, just in case.

From the laboratory door I could see Akiviak climbing down from the landbrink onto the ice in the twilight. He continued out over the landfast ice and ran out of sight behind the first line of hummocks to the north.

Later he gave me an account of his hunt. Beyond this hummock, he said, he came to a flat field of newly frozen ice. He continued across this new ice, moving quickly, up against the wind. As he approached the chaotic jumble of pack ice on the far side of the ice field, a polar bear appeared on the highest hummock straight ahead. It remained standing on all four feet, stretching its long neck and swinging its head in sweeping moves from one side to the other.

Akiviak stopped in the middle of his stride, remained motionless, as there was no cover. The bear turned around and disappeared. Akiviak rushed toward the hummock; he was sure that the bear had seen him and was running away. But as he reached the top of the hummock he could see it swinging its way across the screw ice. It disappeared before he had time to lift his rifle.

Akiviak continued ahead, carefully, following the bear tracks. The hours passed. Then he noticed that the bear had started to scratch the surface of the snow here and there. From experience he knew that this was an indication that it would soon lie down. The tracks made a large curve to the right, across the direction of the wind, as is customary when a bear is about to rest and wants to have the wind down his tracks so that the scent will warn it of any approaching intruder. Climbing up on a high piece of ice to take a look, Akiviak caught sight of the bear asleep in the snow, no more than twenty yards away. Akiviak scraped the ice with his mukluk to awaken the bear, but it remained undisturbed. Then he shouted, the bear lifted its head, and Akiviak pulled the trigger.

It was a skinny bear, Akiviak said. He had barely skinned it when his lead dog came running across the ice. For some reason it had been left at home that day but had broken loose and followed Akiviak's tracks. Akiviak cut a piece of the bearskin and tied it around the dog's neck and told him to run home. Meanwhile he dressed the bear, then sat down to wait. He took a few bites of a stick of frozen caribou meat which he carried tied to his belt. "There is warmth in frozen meat," he used to say.

When the dog reached the village a couple of hours later, Akiviak's sons harnessed the dogs and set out to track him. Upon their return, the women scraped the hide, washed it in soap and water, soaked it in urine overnight, and then hung it to dry on a pole so that it would be bleached by wind and sun.

And then followed another drum dance to celebrate the successful hunt and to honor the hunter.

The next day the schoolteacher, a New Yorker who had married an Eskimo girl, came to inform us that his wife was about to give birth to a baby. We followed him to the "schoolhouse," where he lived with his wife, wondering what had brought a New Yorker up here and what had motivated him to marry an Eskimo girl with whom he had very little in common, and whose language he had not even taken the trouble to learn.

We found the patient in a sleeping bag on top of two wooden packing boxes which were not even of equal height. There was no bed in the house. No one knew for sure when the baby was expected. Following the violent drum dance the woman had felt pains, and now she was having contractions at regular intervals. No preparations of any kind had been made.

In earlier days Akiviak and his wife had served as midwives. I gathered that he knew a great deal about the subject, but this time no one had asked his advice, so he was uninterested. On this occasion it was a younger Eskimo called Apopa who functioned as obstetrician, with the aid of his wife. It appeared that he was well informed too and had had considerable experience. He was able to determine the position of the fetus and could palpate its different parts and extremities. He placed a rope around the chest of the patient, "to prevent the pains reaching the upper parts of her body," as he put it. When he started to squeeze the baby out by applying pressure on the mother's abdomen, I felt it was time for us to take over, and we delivered a bouncing seven-pound girl.

All the children of the village had gathered outside the window, until they were driven away by one of the mothers, but an eight-year-old girl hid behind the door to follow the events at close quarters. The rest of the schoolteacher's family remained undisturbed at the table nearby and continued to eat caribou meat dipped in a cup of seal oil.

The mother smiled through tears at her husband, who looked serious and pale as he took her hand, unable to understand what she was saying to him in Eskimo. One could not help wondering what was in store for this couple and their child, who would probably always face the problem of adjustment, whether they elected to remain among the Eskimos or decided to live among the whites.

The children, and many of the adults too, all of whom had colds, flocked around the mother to see and to touch the new baby; it was difficult to keep them away. It was amazing to us that so many Eskimo mothers and newborns survive under these conditions without the faintest appreciation of even the most elementary principles of hygiene.

According to Akiviak, it is customary for the mother to nurse the baby for a year or two, or until the next child arrives. He further explained that up to the time the missionaries came the young couples "moved to live together by love," as long as the girl was over fourteen winters of age. But they had to know each other well to do so, and the old men were particular in their selection of their sons-in-law, who had to be kind, energetic and good hunters.

Even among the Eskimos opinions vary with regard to the

bringing up of children. "We spank the kids, if need be, and send them to bed, but let them come out again as soon as they promise to be good," explained Akiviak. "In general, we spank them harder each time they repeat the same mischief."

Finally, at the end of a month, the day came when we had completed our studies, had packed all our equipment, and were ready to return to Fairbanks. Akiviak and his bride and his daughter, and their two suitcases, were to accompany us. We piled into the plane and fastened the seat belts. Halfway down the runway, as we were a few feet off the ground, the pilot suddenly cut power, dropped the airplane back on the ground and slammed on the brakes with such force that we skidded all over the runway. It appeared that the air-speed indicator was out of order. It was fixed in a hurry, and soon we were off through a blinding snowstorm across the mountains. We lost radio contact, but continued, and finally started to let down through the blizzard without vision. When we finally touched down at Ladd Air Force Base, we had seldom appreciated being on the ground more.

The Eskimos, who probably still preferred to travel by dog team, took off through the blizzard for their wedding. But Akiviak and Rebecca were never wed. Rebecca was admitted to a tuberculosis sanitarium, and Akiviak returned to the coast and was killed out on the ice.

A preliminary analysis of our findings suggested that these Eskimos, who were quite representative of the Alaskan coastal Eskimos, had a significantly higher rate of body heat production than normal whites. Whether this was due to physiological acclimatization to cold, to the high meat diet causing an elevated metabolic rate known as the specific dynamic action of protein, or to some unknown racial or ethnic factors remained to be seen.

Next on our schedule was Kotzebue, the largest and most civilized of all Eskimo settlements in Alaska. There we would be able to study the effect of the white man's diet, clothing and customs on the Eskimo's ability to survive in the arctic environment. The necessary arrangements had been made with the Alaskan Native Service physician at Kotzebue, who kindly made the hospital facilities available to us and gave us valuable co-operation.

It was still dark as we took off in an overloaded C-47 one Sunday in December and headed west. We continued through overcast until we crossed the Kobuk River and approached the coast. Here the visibility improved and exposed the flat wind-swept barrens and Kotzebue Bay, extending like an ice-covered shadowless field until it blended with the western horizon. We made the approach close to the ground over the village on the narrow Kotzebue Peninsula. There was hardly a sign of life below, only an occasional faint spiral of smoke rising from snow-covered cabins grouped in rows between the snowfans along the beach. A footpath followed the landbrink and led to the store, a plowed road cut through the village, passed the town hall, the church, the cemetery, the schoolhouse, and ended in an open square in front of the hospital.

We skidded on the icy gravel and parked the C-47 at the end of the runway. A biting wind hit us as we opened the door and started to unload the boxes of laboratory equipment onto a tractor sled. We pulled the parka hoods down over our faces and set out across the snowbanks toward the hospital, passing small snow-covered huts along the road, shacks of packing boxes and driftwood, hastily slapped together and covered with sod. Dogs were chained at every house. Skins were stretched out on the roofs to be dried. Half a dozen airplanes were parked out on the ice to our left.

An old woman was fishing for cod through a hole in the ice close to the shore. Sitting comfortably on an empty oilcan, she was handling the line with mittens on, using wooden sticks to manipulate the line without wetting her hands. A child dressed in fur tumbled on the snow around her, playing with a puppy. An Eskimo hunter was watching them from the shore. He wore caribou mukluks, khaki trousers, and a parka made of white fur. The large hood with the wolfskin trimming was pulled over his head, but the smooth skin of his old face was exposed. Only at the corners of his eyes were there wrinkles from a lifetime of squinting against the sun. The eyes were merely cracks in the skin, and the broad chin was completely beardless. As the sun appeared above the hills, it shone in his face. "He looks like a painting on a Christmas card," said Joan as we passed.

Past the schoolhouse the driver ran the tractor into one of the large wind-blown snowdrifts that had formed across the road. The more he tried to back out, the deeper he sank into the snow. Finally, we borrowed a shovel and started to dig the snow from under the belly of the tractor to provide traction for the belts. Every time we sat down to rest the Eskimo took the shovel and removed snow from under the belts too, so we would have to start all over again.

Eventually a large crowd of natives gathered around us; apparently they thought this was funny. One of them offered us the use of his dog team at the rate of $10 a load. But the Eskimo who owned the sled which he proposed to use required another $10 per load, and finally his brother, who would assist him, also was to have some remuneration. So we decided to proceed with the digging.

It took us hours to get loose. As we rattled onward, with our shoulders braced against the load to steady it, half the village followed in a gay procession. By the time we reached the hospital many of our chemical reagents were frozen and the bottles broken. And when we finally had dug our way into the empty hut that was to serve as our laboratory and went to light the stove, the chimney caught fire. The Eskimos, who were still gathered outside, had the time of their lives as the sparks descended upon them like rain. Finally the Eskimo maintenance man was called to our rescue and promptly brought the fire under control.

While we waited for the ice to melt on the windows, we walked over to the "hotel" to arrange for living accommodations. The main entrance was snowed under, so we went to the back door. We crawled up a snowbank and slid on the slippery ice through the doorway and landed on the floor stained with slimy seal oil. Fumbling through the darkness we came upon a large room where an old sourdough with a huge woolen cap on his head was drinking coffee while he argued with an Eskimo who was almost invisible in a dark corner. An aircraft propeller was stuck on one of the walls; piles of parcels and packages of all kinds were scattered on the floor around the stove. An opening in the wall was covered with a piece of cardboard with the inscription: "Closed, come back tomorrow."

This was the local office of the airlines serving the district.

An unshaved cachectic-looking attendant with a tall chef's cap on his head came out from the kitchen with a wooden jack plane in his hand. He greeted us with the remark that it was not easy to be both manager and cook at the same time. When we asked for rooms for a married couple and two single men, he thought for a while. They had only one double bed, he eventually informed us, but it was already taken. He pointed to the corpulent sourdough by the table, who agreed to give up his room to us.

We had dinner at the hotel. The generator had broken down, so we gathered around the kerosene lamp on the table and were unable to see in detail what we ate. One of the guests informed us in a most secretive manner that the cook was heavy on the bottle. In the morning he would, as a rule, be so shaky that whatever was ordered turned into scrambled eggs.

A lantern was placed by the stairs on the first floor. This we grabbed as we climbed up and then it was passed along from one room to the next. We had to move about cautiously because there was a large opening in the middle of the floor, through which the heat, smoke and smells ascended from the dining room below.

The technicians shared a room with three beds. The door was missing, and the opening was covered with a blanket, as was the door leading into the next room, where a noisy party was in progress. A couple of men with some Eskimo women sat on the beds and loudly debated matters that are not normally discussed.

We had found that the best way to establish contact with the natives and to persuade them to serve as subjects for our studies was to approach them through the village minister or schoolteacher, who had their confidence. It turned out that most of the Eskimos were perfectly willing to join us in the winter, when they enjoyed our C rations and the heat of our laboratory. In the summer it was a different matter; for then they wanted to be free to roam as they pleased. The following day, therefore, we went to see the Presbyterian minister, who, with his family, occupied a fairly large house, at least by the local standard. They lived plainly and had many children. The minister was a lean, muscular man with a very serious face. Both he and his wife were quiet, kind and helpful.

He had served among the Eskimos for more than fourteen years. At first he drove by dog team from village to village, now he buzzed around in his single-engine Cessna. "But even so," he said, "after all these years I am still unable to understand these people completely. It is impossible to stamp out their superstitions, even among the young generation." He complained that the Eskimos themselves were aware of the gap between themselves and the white men. "One can always detect their feeling of inferiority," he claimed, "and then it is difficult to gain their confidence. The white missionary, on the other hand, cannot possibly place himself on the cultural and material level of the natives either. And so there is always a distance between us."

He explained that Kotzebue was an old settlement; Eskimo families from the villages to the north and south and from the Kobuk River used to come in the summer and live in skin tents along the beach, while they fished for salmon or hunted narwhal and seal.

"It was lively then," he said. "Now the Eskimos are degenerating. The children no longer speak Eskimo, and English badly enough, for that matter. They are allowed to do as they please. The youngsters play poker, roam around all night long, and sleep most of the day. Once in a while they take a job and earn good wages. Then they are unemployed for several months while they collect unemployment compensation. There is no sense of economy. It is hard to find a family who still is living off the land."

The minister agreed to go with us to visit some of the families he knew in order to explain to them what we wanted. We followed him past the hospital and across the open field north of it, bending our bodies against the wind. The sun stood low in the sky, but still glowed on a shabby canvas tent in the middle of the field before us. The tent was the year-round home of the Nappak family. The thin canvas was stretched over a frame of two-by-fours, with a door on the lee side and a window at either end.

The minister pulled the rope that opened the door. We followed him in, knocked the snow off our parkas, and remained standing on the dirt floor by the stove. The stove was nothing more than one half of an oil drum covered by a sheet of iron; in this they burned fuel oil.

Nine people lived in the tent. Seven of them were lying on the floor, shivering. Two of the children were sitting in a corner fully dressed in their parkas. The older of the boys had retreated far back into the corner. He was thin, appeared alert and embarrassed. The mother, dressed in her parka, arose from the rags behind the stove and settled herself on a wooden box. Tired and pale but rather good-looking, she was visibly pregnant.

Nappak himself was lying closest to the wall. Some of his features resembled those of the Lapps: the protruding chin bones and the lightly colored skin. He had known a number of Lapps in his youth at the time they brought the reindeer into Alaska, and he claimed that his father owned the largest reindeer herd in the district.

The minister had already told us that Nappak's children were hungry and his wife was pregnant every year. Their babies arrived with such regularity that people in the village who could not remember their names referred to them by the year they were born.

This, then, is how these people lived, jumbled together in a flimsy tent, relieving themselves in a can, and hardly ever washing. The children were lying side by side on the drafty floor, fully dressed for warmth. A dark-eyed girl and a handsome little boy, their teeth chattering, had crawled close to each other; they peeped out from under the blanket and looked at us with twinkling eyes and smiled with a charm that would have moved the coldest of creatures. It seemed hard to understand how happiness could thrive and human dignity and love survive under such conditions.

Nappak loved to talk. And he told his tales with humor and charm, resting on his elbow and rolling a cigarette while he talked. His wife just sat there, her hands folded in her lap, looking at the floor. Once in a while there was a flash of a faint smile on her face when the rest of them laughed. Then her dark eyes came to life, and she became a real beauty with perfect white teeth.

We continued through the blizzard, fighting to remain upright as we struggled across the long snowbank by the beach, past snow-covered boats frozen to the ground and empty gas drums. Behind us the sky was still copper red where the sun had set, but in the shadowless twilight it was impossible to see the contours of the ground; the blowing snow into which we were heading hit us in the face and blinded us almost completely.

Finally we reached Okratsiak's igloo, a sturdy cabin of logs with the bark on, and a roof of peat. In the hallway we stepped over a dog with a litter of puppies hanging to her udder. Okratsiak was alone with the children; he was baby-sitting while his wife was at the store, he explained. He could not quite see why she had to go to the store, anyway, he added. He stroked his sparse beard with a finger. The coarse, scanty hair stood straight out and gave him quite a comical appearance. We had been told that a pure Eskimo has no beard and no hair growth on his body with the exception of the top of his head. We found this to be true; in fact, even pubic hair was as a rule absent in the full-blooded Eskimo, and an old Eskimo was highly amused when he saw a painting of a white nude in the schoolteacher's house.

Okratsiak was a likable fellow and a very entertaining teller of tales: "I was born in a skin boat on the Kobuk Lake in the fall at the time of the freeze-up," he informed us, "but we made it to the shore," he added, as if he personally had had something to do with that success.

He and his children had gathered around the table and were eating boiled seal meat and intestines which they dipped in a bowl of melted blubber. The older of his daughters cut pieces of the black meat with a broad knife of the primitive type, made from the steel of a saw blade attached to a handle of walrus tusk. Afterward they had rolls and some tea.

When we offered Okratsiak a cigar he became very jovial and turned unusually talkative. Joan was particularly fascinated by his account of how they had been haunted by wolves in his childhood and how his grandfather used to drive them away with a mitten which he swung over his head by a rope. The wolves would attack the dog team in flocks of up to a hundred. They surrounded the sled in rings, one outside the other, and tore apart everything they could sink their teeth into. When the driver ran out of ammunition he whirled a piece of baleen attached to a string of sinew over his head; the screaming, whining sound thus produced would scare the wolves away.

In a two-story frame house next to Okratsiak's cabin lived an Eskimo by the name of Ohoto who was considered to be the best hunter in the village. We found him sitting at the table eating pancakes with syrup. He was dressed in a pair of skin pants with a zipper at the back. From time to time he looked out through the window to keep an eye on the weather. It was clear that he was impatient. He had been out hunting the day before and came upon a herd of caribou on the tundra, but they were so shy that they vanished before he could come within rifle range. Now he was itching to try again.

His sister sat on the floor busily engaged in the preparation of a sealskin. "They remove the blubber from the skin as soon as the seal is killed," the minister explained. "They rub the hair side of the pelt with ash and scrape off the hair. Then they roll the pelt into a bundle and dump it in a container filled with blubber oil and leave it there to rot. They then soak it in water until the hair side of the pelt is sufficiently bleached, at which time they place it outside and keep it frozen all winter. In the spring it is stretched on a frame and kept in the sun to be bleached further. Finally, they cut the skin in strips and dye them with extract from the willow bark, and use the strips as trimmings on their winter mukluks."

By now the wind had died down, and as Ohoto was getting ready to go hunting we went on in the moonlight along the beach toward the store. We walked past igloos of all shapes and sizes, with whining dog pups in the shadows at every door.

The Eskimos had gathered outside the movie theater, the Midnight Sun, waiting for the door to be opened. For half a dollar they were allowed to stand along the walls to watch the cowboys and cattle thieves thunder across the prairies. They watched in silence, beaming, and every time one of them laughed they all laughed. What they laughed at none of us could tell.

In the store we found the storekeeper sitting on a board across the top of an open barrel of butter. He was a Pole who had started as a traveling salesman, driving a dog team along the coast between Point Barrow and Nome. He bought fur and sold nearly everything. Now he had a fortune, was sitting there on the barrel philosophizing among jewelry and fur, sugar and flour, and all kinds of junk strewn around him on the counter.

"Oh, well," he sighed, and scratched his back, "the tourists say they feel sorry for the Eskimos. But there is no reason to feel sorry for them, I can assure you. They know what to ask for what they do, but they don't want to work. Now, just before the Christmas holidays, they are only interested in doing things for themselves; they are all going to have new parkas and mukluks for Christmas." He said he had paid them in advance to get them to sew mukluks for him; he had even given them the skins and the sinews. That was six weeks ago, but still they had not given him any mukluks.

Joan tried to console him with the fact that there was really no rush since the tourist season was still far off, and we bought some of his pickled herring and continued on our way.

At the doctor's quarters in the hospital we joined the rest of the whites in the village. The doctor, stout and solid as a rock and the only male on the staff, received us from his easy chair on the second floor. Here he entertained regularly, showed movies, played classical music, served the finest liquor, and here many remarkable stories were related. From time to time he had to get up from his chair and dash into the adjacent radio room to answer an emergency call from a teacher in some remote Eskimo village asking for advice—what to do with a child who has a stomach-ache, how to treat a man with a bullet through his arm, or a boy bitten on the leg by a dog.

From the large window in the doctor's living room there was a remarkable view of the village. One could see the entire settlement, the hospital square, the half dozen stores, the schoolhouse, church, graveyard, the street and all the footpaths, and the lights from the windows of every house. Nothing in the village could happen unnoticed from here, neither among the several hundred Eskimos nor among the hundred or so whites, and what one could not actually see one could imagine. One could see where the hunters went and what they brought home on the sled; one could observe the children playing on the fields around the village and the young people dating in the passages among the igloos.

And it was in this room that they told us the stories about

the bush pilot Archie. He did not fly any more, they said, but spent his time sitting behind the picture window in his fancy new house on Ocean Avenue, watching the ice floating by and yarning about his past. The head nurse told us about his last flight to Point Hope. The villagers there had a polar bear cub tied up, and Archie decided he wanted to bring it back to Kotzebue. He bought the bear and pulled it into the plane and tied it to the floor and took off. All went well as long as the weather was good, but as he crossed the hills and encountered turbulence, the air became bumpy and the bear became restless. It broke the rope and started to tear things up. It was a ticklish situation. Archie begged and threatened in vain, and he could not very well let go of the stick for there was no one else to fly the plane. Finally, as the bear became so violent that Archie was barely able to keep the plane on an even keel, he called Kotzebue on the radio.

"Jesus, this is going to be hell. Can you hear how he roars? Yes, it is the bear, he is loose, he has torn the fuselage apart. Jesus, now he is on the door; here he is . . ."

They claim that as he landed at Kotzebue the bear was in the pilot's seat and Archie was standing behind him trying to hit him on the head with a fire extinguisher.

And they told us of love in 30-below weather, accounts of free love among the youngsters in the igloos, and it occurred to me that this was not so different from what I had seen in the northern part of Norway in my youth.

"Yes, indeed," sighed the schoolteacher, and folded his hands across his stomach, "it is a people in decay. With the older generation this proud race is going to vanish. In the younger generation laziness is taking the upper hand. We spoil them with unemployment securities and all kinds of support. Soon they will expect us to insure them against death."

Several others of the group agreed: "They forget their native tongue, abandon their ancient traditions, give up their good fur clothing for the inferior rags they buy in the store, and chew candy rather than blubber."

The teacher said thoughtfully: "There is no way out for a people limited to a strip of icebound land along the Polar Sea. For the second time in a generation, since their first encounter with the whites, they have been engulfed by civilization. The first time, after the whalers pulled out, the Eskimos returned to their ancestors' way of life. But this time the white race is here to stay. It is pushing on to the north; has already reached the shores of the Polar Sea. The remarkable thing is that the Eskimo welcomes the whites; he wants it this way, for he admires the whites and he himself wants to be like them. If we could only teach them hygiene instead of foreign languages, give them confidence instead of a feeling of inferiority, create respect for their own culture and offer them self-reliance rather than dependence."

A Fish and Wildlife employee agreed that the teacher had a point: "The Eskimos are being engulfed by the white man's migration from the south, so it is simply a matter of making the process as humane as possible."

"Nevertheless, there are some Eskimos who believe that their old ways were good enough," the nurse said and mentioned several Eskimos by name. "They feel that the whites are the source of all evils."

"But there are others, particularly among the older generation, who appreciate and value the help they have received," suggested the sheriff, and his eyes became foggy when he quoted old Pootoo: "We are grateful for what the white man has done. I remember my father starved to death; nowadays no one dies of starvation."

The doctor also had an opinion: "The Eskimos have always been pushed; they were forced to the north by the pressure of more aggressive tribes who needed the land they occupied, and so they ended up in northern Siberia. As they increased in numbers they were compelled to migrate in search of food, that is how they came over here."

"This is a people who must devote all its energy simply to maintaining life itself, without any surplus for developments beyond this essential requirement," concluded the sheriff. "That is why their culture has remained as primitive as it is."

"And that is why they succumb without bitterness, this Stone Age people," added the schoolteacher.

In the laboratory our studies progressed according to schedule. As we weighed the food of various Eskimo families, carried out basal metabolic studies in a separate room in our laboratory hut, and analyzed urine and blood samples in the biochemistry laboratory, it soon became apparent that these Eskimos differed from those at Kaktovik. Their diet on the whole was not so high in protein, and their basal metabolism also was lower, though it was still higher than that of our white control group. It began to look as if the high protein content of the primitive Eskimos' diet might explain at least in part their high basal metabolism.

We were curious to know whether these Eskimos showed the same metabolic response to cold as our white controls, and especially whether or not there was any difference in the onset of shiver. For this purpose we exposed nude Eskimos for several hours in a room where the temperature was only slightly above freezing while we recorded their metabolism, their body temperature, and the onset of shiver. This soon developed into a contest among the proud Eskimos to see who could stand the most cold without shivering. I don't recall which of them won, but it turned out that the nude Eskimos outlasted the heavily dressed technician. Our regular tests also showed that the Eskimos could take more cold than the whites, because they produced more body heat.

The days passed, came and went in an endless rhythm of changing twilight. In the morning there was the blue twilight without shadows, then came the dawn of day like a thin copper-colored line over the horizon, gradually extending into a flame covering the entire southern sky until the sun rose above the hills beyond the barrens. The glow lasted for an hour or so, then slowly vanished while the colors remained in the sky: at the skyline a purple-colored ribbon, over it a fainter red which changed into yellow higher up, fading away and blending into the ice-blue sky which blackened above the twinkling stars of the Milky Way.

A dog rose in his chains, stretched his nose toward the sky and howled. It came as a signal, the howls spread from igloo to igloo, dog team after dog team joined in, and soon the entire village was howling under the veil of the northern lights.

4 ESKIMO CHRISTMAS

When Christmas came we were still among the coastal Eskimos at Kotzebue by Bering Strait.

Christianity created this settlement. Less than a century ago Kotzebue was still only a summer camp where coastal and inland Eskimos met late in the spring to barter, to fish, and to dance to the drums. In 1897 the missionaries came and built the first wooden frame house, which became the church. From then on things developed the way they usually do when heathens hear about eternal salvation. They congregated around the church and built themselves igloos of driftwood along the beach. They dug a hole in the ground, piled up logs of driftwood into walls, and covered it all with a layer of sod. Whereas before they had been nomadic people on endless migration, they had now become permanent settlers.

The first missionaries had no difficulty in finding receptive souls among the Eskimos for their preaching of forgiveness and eternal life, because the Eskimos' own faith was rooted in taboos and constant fear of punishment and witchcraft. They were tyrannized by the old shaman, the angakok, who mastered the wicked forces, and respectfully obeyed his most unreasonable demands. When an Eskimo suffered from headache, the shaman would slash the skin of his head, to the accompaniment of grotesque ceremonies and morbid drum songs. Sometimes the patient bled to death.

Today, however, Kotzebue is one of the most civilized settlements in Alaska, with a population of well over a thousand, and with three different varieties of Christianity to choose from. It must be hard for the bewildered Eskimo to make the proper choice, for all three claim a monopoly on eternal life. All threaten their congregation with the devil, which heretofore had been unknown to these innocent souls. And while their forefathers met death with serenity, as the relief which it in reality was, they are now made to shudder in fear of what may be in store for them beyond. The new faith also poses certain practical problems. For instance, the crew of a whaleboat may consist of Eskimos belonging to the different sects, one of which does not approve of hunting on Saturdays, while another objects to hunting on Sundays. Consequently, the crew must remain at home two days of the week, no matter how many whales may be passing by.

Christmas Eve came with a chilly wind from the west, sweeping across the banks of the hard-packed snow along the road by the beach. Dim kerosene lights flickered through the tiny windows of the snow-covered cabins.

Looking out the hospital window we saw a dog team come out of the arctic twilight. We could hear distinctly the scrunching in the snow and the hissing sound of the runners gliding across the wind-whipped crust, the rapid steps of the dogs. An Eskimo was driving the dogs, standing on the runners behind the sled, to which were lashed two Christmas trees. This was Apayaok, who had been up the river to get the trees, one for the hospital and one for himself.

He passed the graveyard on the hill where by the flickering light of a lantern a man was chiseling out a grave in the permafrost. He belonged to a settlement farther north on the coast. His wife had died when giving birth to a child earlier in the winter, and he had brought the frozen body here on his sled. He had been digging all night, for he was in a hurry to get the body in the ground because he had run out of dog food and faced a long journey home. Furthermore, Eskimo tradition barred him from any hunting until his wife was buried.

Down on the fiord ice a woman was sitting on a log fishing for cod. As a bait she used a piece of walrus tusk shaped like a fish, attached to a hook. The line was fastened to a stick which she jerked up and down with the patience typical of the Eskimo. All of a sudden she had a bite. With the aid of a second stick she pulled in the wet line deftly, without having to touch it with her mittens. Carefully she lifted her flapping fish out of the hole and left it to freeze in the snow.

A skinny dog team came trotting in from the bay. This was the thrifty Inuk returning with a seal. He stopped in front of his house, where his wife, the fretful Kunee, greeted him at the door with a grin while her lover slipped out through a hole in the wall.

Old Pootoo appeared on the landbrink to the south with his team of fourteen dogs, heading for his igloo directly across the hospital square. He had been out on the tundra to bring home a caribou carcass for Christmas. The meat had been left buried in the snow since the hunt in the fall. A ring of human footprints in the snow around the cache had kept the wolves away, he explained. He had been gone four days and had spent four nights in the barrens without a tent. He slept in his caribou sleeping bag in the snow, ate frozen meat and drank water which he melted from the ice on the brook by kindling a fire of willow twigs as the Eskimos had done for centuries.

Pootoo was a remarkable man, the old, tough and likable

kind who smiled as a matter of habit and talked continuously. In spite of his age he was straight as a candle, and fit as a youngster.

We went out to help him unload and followed him into his house. It was cozy and warm in the small room with bunks along the walls and shelves above, all the way up to the ceiling. There was a strong smell of burned blubber from the stove. A very old woman was sitting cross-legged on a bunk, filing a thread of sinew between her teeth. Pootoo's wife was sitting on the floor chewing on a piece of sealskin to be shaped into soles for the new mukluks she was making for her husband for Christmas.

As the afterglow faded in the sky, bells in the little steeple on the snow-covered church began to chime. People poured out of the houses, and soon the entire village was on its way to church to celebrate Christmas. That night everyone, irrespective of faith, went to the Presbyterian church which the sober and sensible preacher and his wife had decorated with Christmas trees and glitter.

They came from far-distant places, whole families driving in across the tundra guided by kerosene lamps tied to the sleds. The old ones, too aged to walk, were brought in on sleds pulled by the children. An old blind man with a fiddle under his arm was guided into the church by his daughter.

Most of the people came early. They poured into the church in an endless stream, mothers carrying their babies under the hoods on their backs, old tattooed women in gay cotton-covered parkas and mukluks trimmed with calfskin.

The children ran around among the benches and made a terrible noise, while the adults remained quiet in their seats. Once in a while a screaming child was carried outside to tinkle in the snow. Babies in their mothers' lap sucked on their bottles or were breast-fed.

The preacher stepped forward and requested order in the

hall. Then the choir assembled in front of the stage. The Eskimo conductor with a pair of gold-rimmed glasses on his nose stood in front of the choir and sang an octave or so higher than the rest. He waved his right hand in fancy circles over his head, and on every fourth beat he stretched on his toes and moved his hand in a most elegant sweeping motion around the protuberant breasts of the soloist. And the soloist kept singing, while her little daughter cried at her feet. Suddenly she bent down and grabbed the child and laid it to her breast while still continuing her song.

Finally the show got under way. Cute Eskimo girls with bows in their hair appeared on the stage carrying shepherds' canes. Embarrased and bashful, they read a few lines of the Christmas story, then hurried off the stage while the boys giggled behind the curtains.

The preacher's wife, crawling about on her knees on the floor, was acting as the prompter. By mistake someone stepped on her hand: she yelled and the lights went out. It all seemed to be part of the act.

The show continued for a couple of hours, then they sang a Christmas carol and the arrangement committee, fully dressed in parkas, mukluks and mittens, started to hand out the presents. It was a slow procedure as one by one the villagers came forward to receive their presents—a package of hairpins, a frozen fish that was partly thawed from the heat of the room, a sealskin, a pair of mukluks, a washbasin, an iron, a rocking chair, and four hundred bags of candy. It was late in the night when the congregation broke up and returned to their igloos.

We spent the rest of the evening at the hospital helping the nurses to wrap the Christmas presents for the patients and put them under the trees in the various wards. Long before daybreak jubilant exclamations could be heard from the pediatrics section as the children opened their packages of toys, candy, clothing, and various practical items which the nurses and the physician had gathered. Later they were served Eskimo ice cream, which was considered a special treat. It consisted of melted seal blubber or caribou suet whipped together with various plants and berries, and placed in the snow to freeze.

Later in the morning there were dog races on the sea ice. Everybody who could crawl or walk was there, from the tiniest babies to the oldest man in the village, Jajok, who was so old that he could remember having met the Danish explorer Knud Rasmussen when he passed through Kotzebue on his long sled journey from Greenland.

There were two classes in the dog races, one for men and one for women. The starting point and the end of the trail were marked with huge American flags on poles which were far too short for the size of the flags. Everyone who had a team joined the races and the competition was very keen, for the Kotzebue dogs are known to be among the best in all Alaska. Dogs were fighting everywhere and Eskimos were screaming at the top of their lungs; it was a circus unequaled anywhere.

Later in the day there was a service in the church. In the pulpit, high above the fur-covered congregation, the minister in his plaid jacket spoke slowly and very plainly, using the simplest English. The interpreter struggled so hard that he stuttered in his effort to keep up with the preacher.

"The white man is able to think in words," explained the Eskimo janitor of the church who was standing next to us by the door. "This we cannot do. We think in a series of pictures and actions, and put them together into sentences in our language."

In the afternoon the villagers gathered in the church for supper. Tables were arranged in rows and covered with linen. Each family brought along whatever contribution they were able to make to the banquet: a piece of blubber, maktaq, frozen or dried meat of caribou, seal, walrus or beluga whale, frozen fish, and stomachs of seal filled with berries and other delicacies. They ate and had a wonderful time. The knives whisked back and forth in front of their noses as chunks of meat disappeared down their throats in astonishing amounts. Then some of them burped and all of them laughed.

In the evening they gathered for games in the schoolhouse. The old ones told their tales of the past, and the younger generation competed in physical stunts. And then they danced to the drums. The old people danced and sang while the teen-agers watched. The Kotzebue youths no longer learn the art of drum dancing. Soon it will be nothing but rock and roll with them, and before too long, perhaps, the ancient songs about the hunters of the north, about the whale and the bear and the seal and the deer, with all the humor and ironic flavor so characteristic of this people, will degenerate into a parody number of a circus for the benefit of the tourists.

5 EAST OF THE ICY CURTAIN

Toward the end of February we turned to Sevuokok, a settlement on St. Lawrence Island in Bering Strait, less than forty miles from the eastern shore of Siberia. The St. Lawrence Eskimos originally came from Siberia; their customs and their faith have changed very little from the time of their forefathers.

Here we would have the opportunity of studying one of the more primitive Eskimo groups in Alaska, less affected by the white man's diet and customs than the Eskimos at Kotzebue or Kaktovik. Furthermore, this tribe lived almost entirely on sea mammals, notably walrus meat.

After several unsuccessful attempts to get off during a week of stormy weather, we were finally on our way, with our faithful and dependable pilot, Jim Hammer, at the controls. We flew westward in sparkling sunshine across fields of wind-blown snow along the Tanana Valley, across countless rivers and lakes on the flats where snow-covered beaver houses protruded through the ice; here and there we saw a desolate trapper's cabin at the end of a solitary trail in the snow.

Joan was knitting on a woolen sock, the sergeant, the corporal and 1 were stretched out on the uncomfortable aluminum benches, sleeping, reading or watching the landscape through the scratched plexiglass windows. There is nothing more uncomfortable and uncozy than a GI plane in the Alaskan winter. As a rule the heating system is out of order and it is bitterly cold, or if the heating system happens to work it is almost invariably too hot. All available space is packed with gear, so there is no room to move about.

By the time Joan had completed half the sock we had reached the coast and saw the shore ice extending as a smooth endless fringe along the coastline, in sharp contrast to the irregular pack ice farther out. Beyond the pack ice were fields of newly frozen ice, and finally open water as far as we could see toward the horizon.

We landed on the wind-swept airfield at Nome to refuel, then continued westward over the drift ice. At the edge of an open lead we caught a glimpse of a polar bear hunting seals on the ice. Swarms of eider ducks were swimming in the water between the floes. As we passed overhead they all took to the air and flew across the ice like a cloud of snow flurries with the sun shining on their fluttering wings.

A faint tracing of land appeared on the horizon ahead, the south east corner of St. Lawrence Island, weather-beaten, wind-swept and desolate as an iceberg, locked in the frozen sea between the chilly coasts of Eurasia and America.

The air became choppy, the plane rose and fell, was tossed about and battered by the wind. In moments like these one is reminded that the air is not the most natural element for human existence. The corporal looked pale and serious when he turned to Joan and said, "If we die and end up on a cloud, will you promise to hold my hand?" We followed the coastline and flew in over Sevuokok, a small cluster of octagonal wooden houses along the narrow beach between the ocean and the lagoon in front of a steep mountain slope. On the landbrink facing the sea, rows of skin boats rested bottoms up on tall pillars of sun-bleached whale bones.

With a long harpoon slung across his back, a man dressed in fur was strolling across the ice pulling a dead seal behind him. Dogs were running loose among the houses and people came crawling out of the square doorway openings in the walls as they heard the plane passing over. Another aircraft carrying most of our equipment had already landed, and the crew was unloading the boxes onto the ice of the lagoon. A dog team from the village was heading for the plane.

Our twin-engine plane was jolted about in the turbulent air at the face of the mountain as we circled the lagoon to examine the snowdrifts that had formed like threads across the mirrorlike ice. Because of the strong crosswind the pilot was forced to maintain a fairly high speed, but finally he was able to land on the ice in the middle of the lagoon. He slammed on the brakes, the plane slid like a sled, the pilot struggled with the controls and stamped on the brakes. Every time the wheels hit a snowdrift the plane almost nosed over. At one point it appeared as if we were going to slide sideways onto the shore and crash against the rocks. We closed our eyes and hoped for the best. Eventually we came to a halt just in front of the sheer mountain cliff.

The other aircraft had by now finished unloading and was revving up the engines. Our equipment was piled on the ice and on top of the heap sat our corporal holding on to his briefcase, completely engulfed by the blowing snow whipped up by the propellers.

The items of our equipment that would be spoiled by the frost were loaded on sledges and swiftly pulled by a couple of dog teams to the village. The rest was piled on a huge sled and pulled to the village by a tractor, the sergeant and the corporal sitting on top of the load. Little by little Eskimo children gathered around us, and eventually the dogs joined the parade. They came in hordes, dogs of all kinds and colors, some of them emaciated, carrying their tails between their legs, others well fed, bloody and fierce. On the whole the Eskimos treat their dogs rather poorly, keeping their best dogs tied up, and feeding them as well as they can. The rest of them are allowed to run loose and forage for their own food, which means that the eggs of a parasite known as Echinococcus in the dogs' dropping are spread to human beings, causing the growth of large cysts in the internal organs of the victim.

The sled caravan came to a halt on top of a huge snowdrift running between the church and what had once been the nurse's quarters, which had been made available to us through the kindness of the Alaska Native Service. Now that there was no longer a nurse at Sevuokok, the schoolteacher and his wife had to manage as best they could.

The sergeant placed himself on top of the snowbank, his belly a smooth curved silhouette against the sky, waving his arms as he directed the traffic. The corporal rushed about and had barely time to cough, the long drop under his nose swinging back and forth as he scurried about with the boxes. Joan balanced the five-gallon carboy of distilled water on her shoulder as she strode across the snow crust.

Joan and I were to live in a wing of the church building, which formerly had been occupied by the white minister, who had left several years ago. The rest of the group were to stay in the nurse's quarters, which was also to serve as our main laboratory for the metabolic studies. The rest of the studies were to take place in the schoolhouse.

At first the nurse's quarters made a sad and discouraging impression. Unused for a number of years, the rooms were icy cold, dirty, and filled with snow. The doors had been left open and the dogs had been allowed to enter freely. And there were many dogs in Sevuokok. The Eskimo minister, a tall, slender man with large protruding eyes, came to meet us and solemnly guided us into the church, an old building with an assembly hall and kitchen, living room and engine room all under one roof. He strode like a ghost through the doors, following us like a shadow. Wherever we turned we found him standing there, staring at us.

It struck us from the beginning that there was something strange about this house. It was the oldest building in Sevuokok and had been on fire several times. On numerous occasions some of the older men in the village stopped us in the street and asked if it was true that we were going to live in the church and if we were really going to sleep there during the night. When we said that we were, they looked at us with a puzzled expression. At first we paid no attention to this, but when the schoolteacher told us that that building was haunted we understood their reaction.

At about ten in the evening the minister came to check the motor and to fill the stove tank with fuel oil, then he disappeared. We rolled out the sleeping bags on the pull-out sofa in the living room, locked the outside door, put out the light, and crawled into the bags.

It was not until then that we heard the noises. First there was a squeak in the walls, in the roof, and in the floor, moving from one place to another. Then there was dead silence for a while, followed by a very faint squeak as if someone were tiptoeing across the room; then came a violent bang. We jumped up, startled, looked at each other, and agreed that it must be the old lumber expanding from the heat of the stove.

Then someone rattled the door. "Who can that be?" I asked, and Joan hopefully suggested that probably the wind was shaking it. Something knocked on the window; conceivably it could have been frozen droppings from the dogs blown against the glass by the storm. A light flashed up under the roof, came down along the wall, and disappeared. What else could it be, we reasoned, but the reflected light from the stove, which was visible now that our eyes were adapted to the dark?

In this way we lay there analyzing every noise and every light flash. We closed our eyes now and then, opening one as if to check what we saw. One ghost story after another came to mind. We were almost asleep when we were startled by a crash; it sounded as if a body had fallen to the floor of the loft. Then came a deadly silence. "Are you awake?" asked Joan. "Did you hear that?" I had, and was conscious of a deep chill followed by the flashing heat of fear.

Now something started to knock on the wall, rapid blows as if someone were rapping with his knuckles. Time and time again we crawled out of the bags to examine the wall, listened and flashed our lights into the night. Finally we solved that mystery. Someone had drilled a hole through the wall and hung a framed picture over it. Every time a gust of wind blew through the hole the picture vibrated and knocked against the wall.

The rapping went on all night. It was not so bad once we became used to it, and as the day dawned we lay there in the cozy room, listening to the wind roaring in the stovepipe and the snapping sound of the snow crust as a hunter or a dog passed the church, and watched the light twinkling in the icy crystals on the windows. Then, suddenly, the minister appeared, standing in the kitchen like a shadow, peering into the living room where we slept. We could have sworn that we had locked the door before retiring the night before.

As we were busy preparing breakfast, the sergeant and the corporal came staggering into the kitchen, their faces black as soot, their fingers frozen and white. The stove in their bedroom had exploded in the middle of the night and filled the house with smoke and soot.

And so started our first day in Sevuokok. They turned out to be busy days, for it was a long time since there had been a physician on the island and the Eskimos like to see the doctor. They came to see us with all their complaints. A three-year-old boy had a dental abscess. The Eskimo dentist had been fooling around with the tooth; an abscess causing a swelling from ear to neck was the result. Another boy had smashed a finger under an oil drum, and appeared with blood poisoning involving the whole arm. But most of the Eskimo patients had a multitude of complaints: vague stomach-aches, gall bladder symptoms, indigestion. Accidents and pregnancies were equally frequent.

We gathered that a previous schoolteacher had once studied medicine. It was said that he had gone as far in his studies as the diseases of the heart and consequently he diagnosed cardiac ills rather liberally. When he was summoned for a house call, he would take off with considerable fanfare, dressed in a white coat, his hands, covered with sterile gloves, raised toward the sky. Behind him would come his wife dressed in white and carrying an assortment of boiled syringes in a casserole.

Sunday was a lovely day, with blue sky, bright sun, and blowing snow along the ground. The snow-covered mountains of Siberia could be seen above the drift ice in the arctic mirage. A bowlegged old Eskimo in sealskin mukluks, trousers of sealskin, and a white windbreaker made of walrus intestines over his parka was standing motionless by a weather-bleached whalebone on the landbrink down by the beach, looking out over the ice. The old men spent hours this way, keeping watch for walrus, alone or in small groups on the snowdrifts between the houses, along the landbrink, and on the little hills behind the village.

These people depend upon the sea for subsistence. Over fifty skin-covered umiaks were resting on their drying stands of whalebone and driftwood by the shore. Sun-bleached whale ribs stuck into the ground along the landbrink served as markers for the beaching of the boats. This is where the hunters normally gathered for their lookout. Some of them had been there since dawn that day searching the ice with their field glasses. They were expecting the large herds of walrus any time now as they made their annual spring migration north through the strait. Walrus is the main food staple of the St. Lawrence Eskimo; for him seal meat is only a temporary diet.

The St. Lawrence Eskimos still live largely off the land; hunting and fishing vary with the seasons. They fill their larders during the walrus and whaling season, but may starve during the lean months in the spring before the walrus hunt starts and during the summer before the ice has formed on the sea. Then they often have to get along with a single meal a day.

The main walrus hunt takes place between February and April when the herds drift by on the floes on their way to the Polar Sea. This is the time of plenty, when meat is abundant and everyone is happy. In Sevuokok alone they kill more than three hundred walrus each year.

May and June is the time for the whaling when they hunt the bow-headed whale. Earlier they used to kill at least five of these whales a year; now they are less plentiful and the entire whaling fleet seldom brings in more than three.

During the summer they catch birds and fish, and the women collect plants for food. From June on they gather eggs on the tundra and in the mountains. In the middle of August they start catching the young birds in the rookeries. This continues until the beginning of September, at which time most of the birds start migrating south. By October they have all gone, with the exception of the sea gulls and the ducks which spend the winter on the sea around the island.

The St. Lawrence Eskimos still consume a considerable amount of fish, catching cod among the drift ice early in the year, using nets and hooks. In August they go to Boxer Bay for salmon and trout as they run into the lagoon and up the river. From September on they again fish for cod until the ice forms along the coast. Most of the fish is dried and preserved in seal pokes for the winter. As a rule fish is not used for dog food in Sevuokok.

The seal hunt starts during late summer, when the animals are fat enough to float when killed in the water, and continues day after day until the pack ice covers the ocean at the end of October or the beginning of November. Throughout the winter the hunters keep an eye open for the occasional seal or walrus that happens along, but it is the large-scale walrus hunt in the spring that plays the major role in filling the Eskimos' larders.

As soon as a walrus is killed it is butchered and a piece of the liver and the heart is eaten raw, if the hunter is hungry. If he finds any mussels in the stomach he will eat them too, for they are considered a great delicacy. If the walrus happens to be a female and is fat with much suet around the intestines, he may also eat some of the suet.

The St. Lawrence Eskimos eat practically all of the walrus, with the exception of the bones, the large bowel, the spleen, and the genital organs. The meat is eaten boiled, frozen or dried, or mixed with blubber in the seal poke. The tongue is a delicacy and is eaten boiled. The meat from the head is usually eaten after it is sufficiently decayed to begin to smell. The entire walrus head is kept inside the house for about a week, then the skin is removed and the putrid meat consumed with great delight.

Of the hide, the Eskimos eat the blubber and attached pieces of meat and seem to like it. If the hide is not usable for other purposes, it is rolled up and kept in the underground meat cellar for later consumption. The eyes are boiled and eaten together with the surrounding fat. The brain is removed, frozen, and eaten dipped in blubber oil in the winter; in the summer it is simply boiled. The lungs are suspended from the roof to dry for a week, and are eaten in slices with pieces of blubber like a sandwich.

What part of the stomach is not eaten is dried and used to store anything that has to be kept moist, or for drum skins. The inner lining of the stomach and small intestine is scraped off, kept a few days at room temperature until, like the head of the walrus, it begins to give off a suitable odor; then it is boiled and eaten as a delicacy. The small guts themselves, as well as the large bowels, are used to make rain- and windproof clothing.

The old men claim that if a young walrus is separated from its mother before it has learned to eat as it should it will develop a habit of eating seal, and may even go after people. The angiaracks, as seal-eating walrus are called, are said to be smaller than ordinary walrus, as a rule, and their tusks are short and thick. It is generally known among the St. Lawrence Eskimos that if the liver from an angiarack is consumed, it will cause headache and nausea, and three to five days later the skin will start to peel off all over the body, precisely as is the case when the liver of polar bear is eaten.

The seal is prepared about the same way as the walrus. In the case of the bearded seal, the Eskimos eat the back muscles raw while they are butchering it, and the women scrape the suet from the guts with their nails and eat it.

Of the whale it is the meat, blubber and skin (maktaq) that are considered food. Often they mix it all together and store it in seal pokes for consumption during important celebrations or for emergency rations.

There are certain things the Eskimos never eat, either because they know they are harmful or because they are taboo, such as the liver of the polar bear and beluga whale. "Since the old men never ate it, we do not eat it either" is the explanation they give. Nor do they eat certain shell food, which they know may cause allergic symptoms, fever and nausea, and even choking sensations. Neither do the old Eskimos drink water in the middle of the day. This is a custom that goes back to the time when they "trained themselves to thirst" in case they should drift off to sea on the ice while hunting and not have access to fresh water.

When we arrived at Sevuokok, the food supply was getting low, so all the hunters were watching the ice constantly for signs of walrus. Finally, one day, the message came from the beach. One of the old hunters had seen walrus on the ice on the other side of the open shore lead, and came running toward the house to notify his son. The news was spread by the children from igloo to igloo. The entire village gathered outside the doorways to watch with anticipation as the two large umiaks were carried down to the beach and launched.

An hour later one of the boats returned with a walrus, then came the second boat with two. They landed at the edge of the shore ice, hitched up the dogs, and pulled the umiak loaded with walrus meat and hunting gear over the snow crust up the slope onto the landbrink. There they unloaded the meat, knocked the slush ice off the side of the boat, and lifted it back onto its place on the drying stand with the bottom up.

They shared the catch. The walrus had already been butchered, the hide rolled together like a sausage, and the intestines braided. The skipper of the boat took the head with the tusks, the liver was shared among the crew, and the rest of the animal was divided among the entire population. Then they all went home, pulling the chunks of meat by a rope behind them while the yapping dogs, bloody and torn from their fights, barked and snapped at the pieces of meat left behind.

One morning soon after this we were up before dawn to find that the open lead between the coast and the main body of the pack ice was wide, with scattered ice and large floes beyond it. There was a multitude of water fowl in the open leads: old squaws, eider ducks and black guillemots. Old Tingmiak was standing outside his igloo cutting wood. He was the captain of an umiak and a first-rate hunter.

"Have you seen the walrus out on the ice?" he shouted. Through his field glasses we could make them out distinctly at the edge of a floe a mile offshore, occasionally lifting their heads.

Tingmiak was all set to go out as soon as his son awakened and assembled the entire crew. He said he would be glad to take me along but would be unable to make room for Joan, since his crew of six, plus half a dozen dogs, would take up all the rest of the space. Each umiak has its own captain and permanent crew. As a rule, the captain owns the boat, while often someone else owns the outboard motor. When more than one umiak goes out, it makes no difference which one makes the kill; they all share the meat equally.

The crew gathered at the beach. Tingmiak brought the outboard motor on a sled, and we piled all the gear into the boat: the harpoon with the walrus-skin rope and the seal float, the rifles in baleen containers, ammunition, a wooden box containing a primus stove and some tea, cans of gasoline, ropes, and skins to sit on. When the boat was afloat, the women came running down with the dogs and dumped them on board. This was my first walrus hunt in Alaska, though I had often hunted walrus on the east coast of Greenland.

The 20-foot skin boat is built around a frame of wood, lashed together with ropes of bearded-seal skins. The frame is covered with stretched walrus skins which are split in half after the hair has been scraped off. Aft there is a square hole in the bottom surrounded by a tall wooden shaft. Here they attach the outboard motor, and thus protect the propeller from pieces of floating ice. The boat is steered from the stern.

Two men occupied the seat next to the motor. I sat in front of them amidst the dogs, on a heap of sealskins; the captain stood on the platform toward the bow with his rifle; next to him on the starboard side was his second-in-command with another rifle. In front of them in the bow was the striker, ready with his harpoon, the rope and the seal float. The captain guided all activities with signs. Everyone was shouting and fussing about excitedly; but in spite of the apparent confusion all went smoothly, for each member of the crew had a specific job to perform and knew precisely what to do.

By now a second boat had been launched, and in it I recognized the minister looking very grim. They had already managed to get the outboard motor started and were coming toward us at full speed among the huge pieces of floating ice.

We had trouble with the motor; it refused to ignite. "Soot on the spark plug," diagnosed Tingmiak, and the men got busy with their wrenches. Meanwhile, the captains were calling back and forth in Eskimo, pointing toward the walrus and apparently making a joint plan of approach.

Then we were off. The two ancient umiaks pushed ahead at such a speed that the water foamed in front of the bows; we roared out among the ice from lead to lead under a brilliant sun and between floes covered with glittering crystals of snow. As we advanced, flocks of birds took to their wings and disappeared among the ice. The umiak moved swiftly and easily through the sea, cutting through the shell-thin ice without damage to the tough walrus hide. As we sailed against the sun we could see the waves through the thin transparent skin that formed the side of the boat.

We moved ahead in a zigzag fashion, the captain signaling the course to the man at the rudder. A huge floe directly in front of us blocked our advance. Instead of taking the time to go around it, the Eskimos pulled the boat straight across the floe. This was easy because the umiak had slick, narrow runners of walrus tusks attached under the keel.

By this time the village had begun to come to life as the sun rose over the mountain, and I wondered why the walruses had not been disturbed by the barking dogs and the smoke from the village fires. Earlier the Eskimos had been extremely cautious in this respect, and used blubber lamps which produced no visible smoke; and no window faced the sea, so that no light could be seen from the ocean.

The other umiak made better speed than ours; we could see that it was nearing the ice floe where the walruses were resting. It moved up against the wind, continuing at full speed. There were two walruses still lying at the edge of the ice, but now one of them slid into the water. The other animal remained on the ice, but it seemed apprehensive, raising its head frequently and looking toward the approaching boat. As the two gunmen lifted their rifles to their shoulders, the walrus raised its head again, wobbled toward the edge of the floe, and plunged into the water before the umiak could come within rifle range. The gunmen stood up in the boat ready to shoot, but the walrus did not come to the surface.

The crew of the boat waved at us and indicated by signs which way the walrus had gone. We took up the pursuit. Suddenly the grim face of the walrus shot out of the sea close in front of our boat. The black head, the red, congested eyes, the guard hairs, and the glistening tusks were exposed for a fraction of a second. Then came a splash so violent that the sea sprayed into the boat, and then it was gone.

Now the hunt really started. The walrus surfaced again to starboard; the men fired but missed. They missed again twice before the walrus retreated under the thin, newly frozen ice. We could distinctly see it smashing its head through the ice each time it came up to breathe. We followed its route for a while, but the tough new ice cut into the hide at the bow, so that we were forced to give up.

We pulled in at the edge of an old floe, melted fresh-water ice, and brewed a pot of tea over the primus, while the captain climbed up on a hummock to take a look. By this time we were so far out at sea that we could barely distinguish the smoke from the village. To westward the sun shone on the silent mountains of Siberia. The ice around us was flowing with the current southward, silent and lifeless.

We had lost sight of the other umiak, but when we heard shots we realized that the crew had encountered game. Quickly we all gulped the boiling-hot tea from our tin cups, gathered the gear hastily into the boat, and shoved off. The tiny outboard motor crackled like a machine gun, and the noise rang out over the ice. The cold breeze chilled us to the bones, as we sat motionless in the boat.

As we rounded the protruding edge of an old hummock we caught sight of a bearded seal on a floe in front of us, its head raised and facing us. Tingmiak fired, the head of the seal hit the ice, and did not stir. The Eskimos did not even take time to skin it; they simply pulled it on board and continued in the direction of the shots we had heard.

The ice grew more scattered as we went on, with broad leads of open water between the flat, smooth floes. A dark object became visible on a floe far away. The captain used the binoculars and said it was a walrus. It was a big one, he thought. He could tell from the appearance of the snow on the ice that very recently there had been several walruses together on the floe.

The direction of the wind was in our favor, so we headed straight for the walrus and sought cover behind hummocks and large pieces of pack ice until we were so close that we could distinctly see its tusks each time the walrus lifted its head. Then we cut the motor and started to paddle, two men on each side. Every time the animal raised its head, the Eskimos rested their oars and did not move. We were now so close that we could see its eyes. It was on the very edge of the ice, and had obviously seen us already, but it seemed to take little interest in us. Both riflemen sat ready, but apparently the range was still too far. After all, they had to knock it out with the first shot. By this time we no longer had any cover; only a stretch of open water separated us from the walrus.

The walrus lowered its head onto the ice; the Eskimos paddled still another few strokes. Everything was so quiet that we could hear the waves ripple against the side of the boat. Then the walrus sank the ends of its tusks into the ice, supporting itself on them while it lifted its head and turned its eyes towards us, so that we could actually see the fiery red fold around the eyeball. A slight grunt escaped from Tingmiak, and the shots rang out simultaneously from both rifles. A visible shock traveled through the huge body, then the head dropped onto the ice, and the Eskimos paddled for all they were worth.

As the boat hit the floe, the walrus came to life. The man in the bow thrust his harpoon into its back and leaped onto the ice while holding the end of the harpoon rope to prevent the animal from sliding into the water. Nevertheless, the huge mountain of meat slowly slid into the sea while the captain fired one bullet after another into its neck. It was a close call, but finally the men succeeded in killing it and fixing it securely to the floe with the aid of an anchor.

Now the real labor began. Four men struggled with the tough walrus hide, while two men were kept busy sharpening the knives for them. Finally, they butchered it and spread the meat out on the snow to cool, and then loaded it in the boat. We started on the long journey back, sitting on top of the pile of meat and shivering from cold. Even the Eskimos dressed in their skin parkas and pants were so cold their teeth chattered.

On occasions like these I was apt to wonder whether it was really necessary for Joan and me to choose a way of living that entailed such miserable suffering or whether it would not have been just as profitable scientifically to study the physiology of the Tahitians. Although the Eskimos' clothing of fur has an insulating value about three times greater than that of the ordinary GI clothing we used, we found it generally impractical to convert completely to native dress because of the inconvenience when we were working indoors, the annoyance of shedding hairs, the obnoxious smell, and the difficulty of keeping fur garments dry. However, we nearly always used fur mukluks in order to keep our feet warm.

I was thinking longingly of Tahiti when, at last, the village came into sight at the foot of the mountain; we could see the boats on the stands along the beach and the igloos behind them, and the smoke that rose into the frosty sky flaming in the setting sun. The entire village came to meet us at the edge of the shore ice, to help us beach the boat and to collect their share of the meat, and two hundred-odd dogs came to lick the blood from the snow.

6 SAVOONGA

Early one morning the radio station operated by the school teacher brought an alarming message of medical emergencies in Savoonga, a small settlement fifty miles farther south on St. Lawrence Island. A small boy had broken his arm, five persons were said to be suffering from pneumonia, and more than half the school children were in bed with flu. Three dog teams were ready to drive to Sevuokok for help. Could we come?

That same evening the dog teams arrived with empty sleds. They were the three best dog teams in Savoonga, but even so they were not in very good shape, for dog food had been scarce during the winter. They came rushing down the mountain and across the lagoon; the drivers were soaked in sweat but their faces were covered with rime frost.

Nasak was the oldest of the drivers and by far the handsomest. Because he was also said to be the most dependable, he was picked to transport Joan on his sled. Ukalek was young and sturdy, with a few sparse patches of beard on his cheeks. He had the strongest dogs and was to take me, since I was the heaviest. The third driver, Amarok, was to follow with the baggage.

The distance we had to travel was about fifty miles as the crow flies and would take us about twelve hours. We set out before daybreak. The drivers had been housed by friends and relatives, who had prepared a few rations for the journey such as coffee and meat which they now carefully put in the skin bags and tied onto the sled.

Nasak came by to see if we were adequately dressed. He offered us a couple of sealskin parkas which we said we did not need. He helped us inflate a rubber mattress which we lashed to the sled, placed Joan on it, tucked into a sleeping bag, and tied the bag to the sled with a rope.

Then the dogs were harnessed and hitched up in pairs, attached to a long walrus-skin rope running between them, the lead dog in front by himself. By this time the entire village was up and about, stumbling around in the twilight offering a helping hand as needed. The dogs, beside themselves with enthusiasm, rose on their hind legs and threw their full weight into the harness, stretching the ropes like violin strings. The moment the sled was freed they surged ahead. As always during such a start, the team galloped wildly across the snowdrifts with the dancing sled seeming to fly through the air.

The sun rose as we reached the edge of the landbrink and down on the ice of the lagoon ahead of us we caught sight of the dog team with our baggage, winding its way among the snowdrifts. Our lead dog, who apparently could not stand to see any other team ahead, let out a yelp, and leaped into the air. In a mad gallop we raced down the slope and sailed in complete chaos out across the bare ice. The Eskimo drivers yelled, waved their arms in despair, and started to throw snowballs after their dogs, since they had no whip with which to control them. This, apparently, was a practice that the missionaries had forced them into; they objected to the Eskimos' driving their dogs in fan formation, as they used to do, because that allowed the driver to reach each individual dog with the whip. Driven in tandem and undisciplined by a whip, the dogs became all tangled up in the ropes; the driver lost control of the team, and in desperation resorted to throwing snowballs or stones at the dogs to force them the way he wanted them to go.

The harness was made of sealskin, with bone or wooden buckles. The sled was light, with runners of steel or walrus tusks. Tied to the stand in the rear of the sled were the sled bag and the anchor, behind which the driver stood on the runners, using as a brake nothing more than an iron spike which he pushed into the ground with his foot. From time to time he would jump off the sled to run behind it, or kick with one leg to help the dogs push ahead.

Once in a while the driver reached down to pick up a lump of hard-packed snow which he hurled at a dog that failed to pull properly. The victim let out a yelp and pulled like mad for a while. One of the dogs was trying to relieve himself, but the driver had no intention of stopping to give him a chance. The poor animal continued to run on his forelegs as he was pulled along by his harness, his hind legs hanging in the air.

By this time the entire convoy of dog teams had fallen into line and we were proceeding in an orderly fashion. Nasak was in the lead with Joan, followed by Ukalek and his team, and finally Amarok with the baggage. Looking back we discovered another sled, and behind it on the slope by the village still another; altogether five sleds pulled by seventy dogs were heading for Savoonga that morning.

The last two teams belonged to Sevuokok. One of them was driven by a hunter who was heading for a cabin midway between Sevuokok and Savoonga; the second by a young boy who was on his way to propose to a girl in Savoonga. It seemed that there was a surplus of seven men in Sevuokok, and all the mature women there were already married or spoken for.

It is a strange sensation to travel on a dog sled across the sparkling snow fields in the sunshine. We slid across shadows of the mountains on the snow, not a sound but the hiss of rapid footsteps of the dogs, and the friction of the sled runners on the snow surface. The animals, obviously in a gay mood, varied between trot and gallop, jerked the rope and sent the sled dancing across the smooth mirrorlike ice.

The teams varied their pace, moved up alongside each other. At times it looked as if they were running in step, side by side, with their tongues hanging out, panting, and kicking up the snow with their paws. Lumps of snow flew at us, as if we were traveling through a blizzard, and we had to protect our faces with our hands. Some of the dogs pulled sideways, others pulled straight ahead, and some of them just trotted along without pulling at all. Each dog ran in his own characteristic fashion; some were stiff-legged, others were graceful and fluid. They were surrounded by a fog of condensed moisture or ice particles, and there was a rim of hoarfrost in the pelt around their faces. Once in a while one of them would get a lump of snow stuck between his toes and struggle frantically to get rid of it, for, if left, it would turn into ice and hurt his paw.

The Eskimos themselves were quite impressive; standing silent on the runners in their shiny sealskin trousers and fancy mukluks with a ring of hoarfrost framing the hoods of their fur parkas, they looked like creatures from another era, searching ahead along the trail by the sea, observing every minute detail in the behavior of their dogs, ready to act instantaneously with punishment or reward as the situation might require.

They had traveled this path many times, as had their forefathers when several thousand Eskimos inhabited the island. The way of life had always been the same, even though the techniques might have changed. They used to travel with the entire family on the sled, which at that time was lashed with sealskin ropes. Now the sleds were nailed and held together with iron screws, and as a consequence were rigid and awkward.

With the village and the lagoon well behind us, we left the coast and cut inland, up the slope toward the mountains on the north end of the island. The snow was wind-blown and hard, so the going was good.

From the summit we had an unobstructed view of the entire coastline eastward, with the landfast shore ice and the pack ice beyond it. In front of us there was a large lagoon several miles long. Here and there logs of driftwood stuck up through the snow, twisted roots and weather-bleached trunks of trees brought in by the Yukon River. Farther inland rows of whale ribs pointed toward the sky, monuments of the whaling age when steel and iron were introduced to this Stone Age people, given to them in exchange for use of their native women. Some undesirable habits accompanied this change. The minister had told us that the Eskimos, trading sealskins for barrels of rum, would stumble around intoxicated while the walruses and the whales passed by unnoticed in the spring. Starvation and decay were the result.

We continued down the slope toward the coast at great speed. The drivers used their brakes, the dogs raced in a wild gallop across the snow crust, and it was all we could do to hold on to the sled.

Down below at the end of a ness there was an old igloo surrounded by several tent frames. On the landbrink an umiak was turned upside down on a stand made of whale bones. I thought this must be a summer camp where the Eskimos came to fish and hunt and hoped that the drivers would tell me something about it but, as is their way with strangers, they were uncommunicative.

The story of Tingmiak and his two wives in Sevuokok came to mind. The minister had conveyed to him that polygamy was not quite compatible with Christian ethics. However, a more

The author and his wife at Sevuokok, St. Lawrence Island

Joan Rodahl and Corporal Blakely sweeping snow out of the Jamesway hut laboratory at Kaktovik

Drum dance
at Kaktovik

Eskimo boy at Kaktovik with polar bear cubs. He is wearing a cotton-covered caribou skin parka with wolverine trimming and caribou boots, the soles made from skin of a bearded seal.

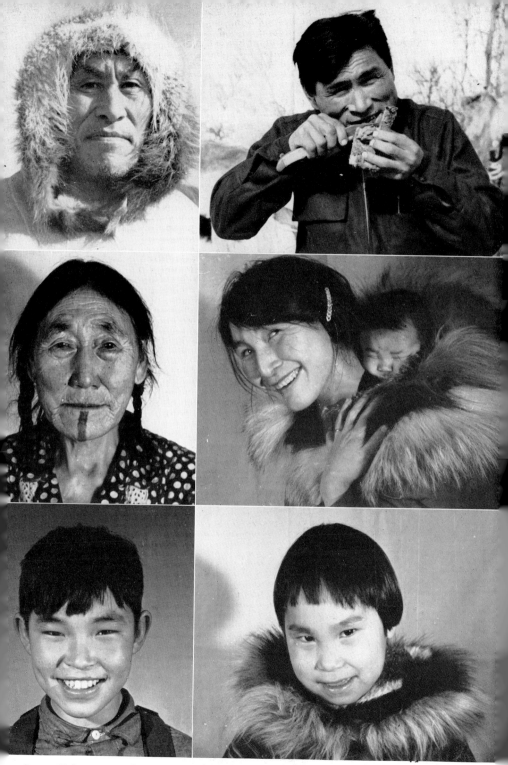

Some Eskimo friends

Houses at Kotzebue (above) and hospital (below)

Beaver aircraft in Anaktuvuk Pass in the Brooks Range

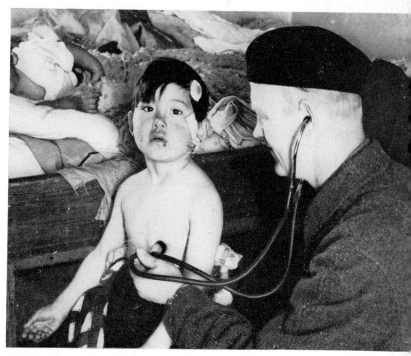

The author with Eskimo boy

Old Eskimo hunters at St. Lawrence Island, scanning the sea ice for walrus

These Eskimos have just shot the walrus seen in distance on ice floe

*Eskimo children
with dog sleds*

Dog sled caravan on the way to Savoonga

Eskimo family in front of their skin tent in the willows at Anaktuvuk Pass

Interior of tent, which is made of caribou skins stretched over a frame of willow branches, with window of seal gut

Meat cache at Anaktuvuk Pass, also occasionally used as a winter morgue

The log cabin covered with peat has now largely replaced the old skin tent

Hunter at Anaktuvuk setting off on a sheep hunt with pack dogs

Joan Rodahl with Eskimo children

The author vaccinating Eskimo child, assisted by local postmaster

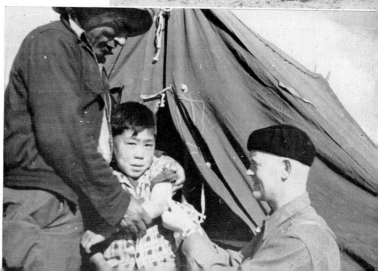

Salmon fishing camp at Kotzebue Sound in the summer

Slaughtering the beluga whale, brought in after a night's kill, Kotzebue

Eskimo women drying skin of narwhal

Seal pokes used in hunting walrus and whales. Tied to a harpoon, the poke hinders the animal in its attempt to dive

Seal rookery on St. Paul,
Pribilof Islands, at
height of the mating
season

Old Eskimo with seal
harpoon and tackle at
Sevuokok

Eskimo skin boat (umiak) in the making. Very few Eskimos have the skill to build these any more.

The author (By *Life* photographer George Silk © Time Inc.)

penetrating examination of the Eskimo way of life suggests that this business of having more than one wife may not be as immoral as would appear at first glance. It was really a practical arrangement, similar to the acquisition of a maid in our society. Since only the most prosperous hunters could allow themselves such a luxury, polygamy was a sign of prosperity and wealth. To start with, Tingmiak had only one wife and with her he shared everything. As in time it became apparent that Mrs. Tingmiak no longer could cope with all her domestic chores singlehanded they agreed that a wife number two should be provided. And it was the old Mrs. Tingmiak who made the selection. She picked, as could be expected, a hard-working female without any sex appeal. Thus old Mrs. Tingmiak had more time to devote to her husband and his needs, and they were all very happy. But then the minister appeared and insisted that one of the wives had to go. Tingmiak felt, however, that he needed them both, so finally he came up with the idea of arranging for a formal divorce from his old wife in the spring, so that he could take his younger wife along to the summer camp, while his old one would be free to remain at home in Sevuokok. When he returned in the fall he simply divorced his younger wife, remarried the old one, and allowed the former to live in his house as his guest. Thus all parties were satisfied—and this is just about as deep as the Christian faith has penetrated into the minds and affairs of some of these people. Although they faithfully parade to church every Sunday with a Bible in their hands, by and large they will retain the faith of their forefathers and adhere to their traditions.

We continued along the coast in perfect weather. A dog team pulled up beside our sled, fourteen dogs in pairs cruising by at an even rhythmic pace. The driver was standing at the back, a foot on each of the runners. This was the bachelor who was on his way to propose to the girl. He was anxious to get there and was driving lightly with an empty sled. Passing the other sleds, he turned to look back and gradually dropped out of sight. The rest of us continued with all four teams spread side by side over the field.

Finally the drivers decided to talk, and from then on they talked almost continuously, asking about all sorts of things in a fairly fluent English. They informed us that considerable competition and jealousy existed between the two settlements. Sevuokok had an excellent location out on the point. Usually there was open water; if the wind was from the north, there was open water on the south side of the point; if the wind blew from the south, there was open water on the north, and open water means the congregation of walruses, seals and birds.

Savoonga, on the other hand, had been founded more or less by chance, or by force of circumstance. To start with, it had been merely a slaughtering place for the reindeer herds on the island, a remote site that the owners of the herds had purposely moved to in order to escape interference by the rest of the people of Sevuokok. Thus some sort of summer camp grew up at Savoonga. When later the herds started to migrate, the men followed them as shepherds while the women remained in Savoonga. Eventually, the reindeer starved to death and the herders were forced once more to turn to the sea for a livelihood, but in this respect Savoonga was not ideally located.

Continuing along the coast, the dog team caravan wound its way, through a jungle of pack ice, around a sheer cliff rising from the sea, across a ridge on a ness. On a hill we came upon a cabin where we were to rest and have a meal. The young bachelor was now far ahead. He disappeared as a tiny speck out among the ice as we pulled up at the hut.

The dogs curled up in the snow. We pulled Joan out of the bag, untied the sled bag with the food, and waded through the snow up to the hut. The floor of the hut was made of driftwood, splintery, dirty, greasy and slippery. In the corner there was a bed covered with a mattress of reindeer skin; an oil drum placed on some blocks of wood served as a stove; the rest of the room was filled with junk: old mukluks, a pair of binoculars without lenses, a shoulder of a walrus, some seal blubber, a tin can to melt snow for drinking water, and a smaller can that served as a chamber pot.

We tried in vain to get the fire going in the oil drum, sipped coffee from the thermos and ate some frozen bread with cheese and ham. We were shivering, and the fingers holding our sandwiches were so cold that they were blue. Then the Eskimos placed the tin can on the table with a smile and, telling us to take our time, crawled out through the hole in the wall into the snow.

We felt more frozen when we continued our journey than when we had arrived at the cabin. The dogs trotted along in the pale sunshine; a hail of snow hit us in the face, mixed with dog droppings and the nauseating scent of digested seal oil and rancid blubber. The driver was in a better position, standing high on the runners, bowlegged and happy, talking to the dogs.

Here and there we passed piles of logs which the Eskimos at one time or another had pulled out of the sea. I asked why they did not throw some of the wood on the sledge and bring it home for firewood. The answer was that there was no point in that, because then the neighbors would help themselves to it, and burn it. As a result of this reasoning, they simply sit and suffer the cold during a storm, and as soon as it is over they may go out to bring home just enough wood to cover the need for that day. This is the Eskimo way.

Nevertheless, it is almost unbelievable what these Eskimos can do if they have to, although they prefer not to. On the whole they are exceptionally well built, with well-developed muscles and rarely any subcutaneous fat, well trained from childhood by their everyday activities. All of a sudden they will jump off the sled to run behind the dogs for a while; then after a brief rest on the sled, they will run again. This is only play for them, and they keep it up mile after mile. They run with a remarkable technique, their trunk swinging from side to side, their legs moving in smooth rhythmic motion. Their mukluks seem barely to touch the ground as they run without effort and without shortness of breath.

We pushed on through a landscape of flat fields and ice-covered lagoons. Then the going became more hilly again, until a mountain range appeared before us, extending all the way to the sea. On the sunlit slope ahead of us we could see a cluster of sod-covered huts, surrounded by skin boats resting on high stands. "My igloos," explained Ukalek. This was his trapping ground. He had inherited the huts from his father, being the eldest son.

We were now only a couple of hours away from Savoonga. The excitement of the Eskimos was apparent as they drove the dogs ahead with renewed vigor. Ukalek's team was no longer able to keep up with the rest; it kept falling behind though we jumped off and ran up all the hills to lighten the load. Ukalek fumed and yelled.

At this point we left the coast and cut inland, due east across the mountains. To our left the cliffs fell straight to the sea; beyond them the strong ocean currents made the ice unsafe. Ukalek, who had been exceptionally friendly and calm, became quite irritable. He was running most of the time and began to throw lumps of snow and ice at the dogs that failed to pull, but they could not keep up.

It was still sunny, but now so cold that I too had to jump off the sled and run in order to keep warm. The icy wind bit at my nose. I had to keep rubbing it with my hand, and my feet were cold in spite of the caribou mukluks. We continued over a hilly terrain, up and down the slopes, across hard-packed snow and bare ground; sparks flew as the runners scraped through gravel and stone.

Far out on the ice we caught sight of a tiny black spot; it moved up and down, from side to side, at times seeming to stretch into a long vertical line, in the next instant shrinking into a spot again. Gradually, it became bigger until we could discern the sketchy outline of an approaching dog team. Our dogs became excited, panted and hissed, braced themselves in their harnesses and pulled with renewed vigor. The teams came together out on the ice in a furious fight. The drivers shouted and yelled, stamped on their brakes and fought among the dogs.

There were two men on the sled, a young boy and an old Eskimo with glasses. The old man had fractured his arm while hunting on the ice. When he returned to Savoonga, he learned that his wife had been taken to Sevuokok to be flown from there to the hospital in Kotzebue, and he was trying to catch up with her in Sevuokok to see her off. "You never know when she will be back," he said with a smile.

I attended to his broken arm as best I could and asked for his name, but he seemed to be embarrassed and did not answer. Finally the boy answered for him. Later we learned that it is considered taboo among some of these people to mention their own names.

Once again we took to the mountains and then down toward the coast on the other side, heading at full speed toward what appeared to be a sheer cliff. Suddenly a narrow cleft appeared, and we made for it. Far below us was the ocean and the pack ice.

I grasped the edge of the sled in a firm grip, Ukalek stamped on the brake, and we were on our way down the mountain. The wind whistled past our ears, and the snow was flying as in a blizzard. The dogs were barely able to keep clear of the sled. We bounced and jumped, once in a while we flew through the air, and only the brake iron touched the ground.

Finally we were down on the plain and continuing across

hummocks and screw ice and open leads on a fiord, and again over land on the other side. On top of the hill there was a graveyard and from there we could see a collection of houses along a beach. "Savoonga," said Ukalek, pointing, and when we approached the village we were met by hordes of dogs.

We drove up in front of a sod hut in the middle of the settlement. The entire village was gathered there, old and young, women with babies under their parkas, and young girls giggling in the background, chewing energetically on their bubble gum. An old man guided us through the crowd to the schoolhouse, where we were to stay. In his broken English he made us understand that they were glad that we could come. The reception alone was enough to thaw our frozen souls; for a moment we almost felt as if we were rendering charity and were doing some good for mankind.

The urgent plea for help over the radio had led us to believe that our arrival was a matter of life and death. It soon appeared, however, that there was no real emergency at all. The teacher merely needed someone to talk to. We had thought that the three Eskimos had come to Sevuokok out of sheer self-sacrifice to fetch medical aid to their suffering brethren, and we had been deeply touched. Later we learned that the drivers had demanded $10 each, and that the teacher, the store, and a community fund combined had provided the money. The Eskimo is perhaps not so different from his white cousin, after all.

We staggered into the schoolhouse with our baggage, almost frozen, our mukluks coated with ice. The teacher and his wife received us, looking pale and nervous. Their little daughter stood behind them, thin and frail under the yellow light of the kerosene lamp, staring into the dark.

Even the coffee was pale. While we had our supper the couple talked to us constantly, both at the same time, about different subjects, with complete disregard for each other.

Then the patients began to come in, seeking advice for all kinds of ills, and almost all of them complained about stomach-ache. "Constipation," diagnosed the teacher, and insisted that it was due to their diet. They ate far too much meat and not enough blubber, and they were hypochondriacs, all of them, he informed us. "And this is all thanks to the nurse who used to live here," he continued. "She gave them all these ideas." Then he told us about an Eskimo who had had an epileptic fit in the church. The following day six other Eskimos had appeared with symptoms of epilepsy.

The Eskimos continued to pour into the dispensary, one after the other, with eye ailments of all kinds, conjunctivitis, scleritis and keratitis. The teacher had the theory that all the eye trouble was caused by irritation from the hairs of the trimming on the parka hoods. One man was blind in one eye and was going blind in the other eye from cataract. He was the postmaster and carried the mail by dog team between Savoonga and Sevuokok twice a week.

And then there was scabies, gall bladder trouble, kidney stones and indigestion. More than a quarter of the inhabitants suffered from tuberculosis in various forms. An old man had a huge hydatid cyst in the liver which was draining through his abdominal wall.

More than half the population was in bed with influenza. We grabbed a flashlight and started on our house calls, walking in the moonlight through the village between the mountain and the sea ice. Arriving at a wooden hut on a hill, we crawled through a square hole in the wall into a hallway full of pregnant dogs, pups, meat and blubber, old hides with a rotten odor, bones, hunting gear and pots of urine. In a corner a ladder led up to a second floor. There three families lived in a single room. They were lying on mattresses on the floor. This was their winter quarters; in the summer they moved down into the rooms on the first floor.

We went from house to house finding our way through the holes in the wall with the aid of the flashlight. Most of the houses had only a single room, though some had two, a front room used in the summer and a second room at the back used during the winter.

The Eskimos had cleaned up in anticipation of our visit. Many of the houses were spotlessly clean, with white scrubbed floors and cloths on the tables. We saw a terminal tuberculosis patient lying in a bed, drawing pictures on a piece of paper. His mother sat on the floor in front of the bed sewing on a pair of mukluks. His father was carving a walrus tusk under the lamp in front of the window.

We were called to see a man who was said to be paralyzed. We found that he had been in bed for over a year. He was emaciated and his legs were very thin. His condition had come upon him suddenly, he told us, when he had caught his wife being unfaithful, and she left him. Upon further examination we found that he was not paralyzed at all, but had convinced himself that he was and refused to leave the bed.

The following day the community council, consisting of the older men in the village, placed an interpreter and a runner at our disposal. Then the teacher brought in a couple of unmarried women who, according to his judgment, were pregnant. They themselves had no complaints at all. They seemed happy and felt well and denied that they were pregnant as a matter of principle. One of them had been regarded as the ideal virgin, an example of virtue and innocence in the village, and had been closely tied to the mission as some sort of Sunday-school teacher. However, it had eventually become apparent that she was pregnant and since conception by the Holy Ghost was not very probable, even in Savoonga, she had been dismissed in disgrace. Another girl was elected to fill her place. It turned out, however, that the new candidate too was pregnant and had been at the time of her appointment.

The teacher had a keen nose for anything that had to do with sex. "The Eskimos are supersexy," he said, standing by the window watching the teen-agers playing about in the snow.

At this point the attractive young missionary passed the window, her blonde hair flying in the wind. There had to be something wrong with a girl who could devote herself to an assignment in a place like Savoonga, suggested the teacher. She held so many religious meetings that they interfered with school activities. It would be more important, he thought, to teach the Eskimos good habits of personal hygiene and, above all, to make them realize that many of their own ancient traditions and practices were far better than the new ones.

"The missionaries have taught them to drive their dogs in tandem, with the result that they now have to use many more dogs to get along, which means more dog food," he went on. "They are proud of the fact that they have persuaded the Eskimos to get rid of their skin tents, in which they lived comfortably all winter long without using much fuel. In the summer they moved out, pulled off the skins and allowed the sun and the wind to dry the peat and to air it all. In the fall they again moved into a dwelling which, by then, was as good as new. Now they live in their wooden houses all year long and the filth accumulates year after year. Only a few of them still use blubber lamps. They would rather buy fuel oil in the store for fifty cents a gallon." Joan and I murmured our interest.

"Many of them have scabies, and fleas thrive in their body-heated fur," the teacher continued indignantly. "Infant mortality is high. Not long ago seven of nine mothers died during delivery, and four of them were sisters. A terrible hysteria was perhaps to be blamed for most of this, for even before they were delivered the midwife and the women started to weep and almost frightened the women to death. Now we have started to give them vitamin pills and have had no trouble since."

It occurred to us as we listened that it is no simple task to transmit the white man's culture to these people.

In the evening Jakob, the senior member of the council, brought a cigar box filled with ivory carvings which he gave us a present on behalf of the people, as a token of their gratitude. He had been elected to take us back to Sevuokok.

We should have started at dawn the next day, but it began to snow during the night and by morning it was blowing a blizzard. All day long we walked from one window to another, waiting. We talked to everyone we could reach on the radio, but all we heard was forecasts of storms everywhere. As soon as the wind subsided enough for us to get out, we went to see Jakob. We found him sitting on the floor smiling and drinking tea, while his wife mended his sealskin trousers. The wind had blown down the chimney and scattered soot all over the room, but no one paid any attention to this.

Jakob appeared to be a wise and quiet chap, stocky and well fed. He had a high-pitched, piping voice and had the habit of saying "yah" at the end of every sentence, making it sound like a period.

He looked up toward the mountains where one could see the moving cloud of blowing snow against the sky. He feared the weather up on the mountains.

"This is the worst kind of wind, yah. It is much stronger up there, yah. My father and three other men drove their dogs over the edge of the cliff in weather like this, yah. And they had the old teacher and his wife too on the sled, yah. You should go and talk to Pujok, yah. He knows much more about the conditions there than I, yah."

We went to see Pujok, a peppy and bouncing little fellow, who seemed almost too arrogant to be an Eskimo. He had more beard growth than most of the Eskimos, which they said was a sign of mixed blood. They also said that he could consume a whole seal in a single meal.

The weather was bad, he said, that was true, and if we wanted to go we had to take the responsibility ourselves. The Eskimos had clothing which kept the cold out, so they could take it all right; but he could not tell what would happen to us. In addition, his dogs were in poor shape; he was afraid they might suffer frostbite on their legs and under their bellies.

The storm quieted down toward evening, but a new low pressure was under way. Nevertheless, Jakob agreed to leave at 3 A.M., for we had heard over the radio that there was a child with acute appendicitis in Sevuokok and this was something the Eskimos respected. Jakob himself had had a girl who died from appendicitis.

It was not yet three o'clock when Jakob came to call us. The Eskimos were already up and busy, the women and the children and everyone old enough to crawl. They waded through the high snowbanks and gathered around the sleds, scampering about, carrying various items of equipment, shouting and fussing and making a great commotion in an effort to straighten things out in the darkness. It was chaos. The dogs barked, people yelled, and we could not see anything. Jakob galloped back and forth, bowlegged in his stiff sealskin trousers, which his wife had just finished. His rifle was slung across his back, and it kept knocking him on the head as he wobbled along. He complained about his dogs, and had to borrow eight from his brother for the trip.

The schoolteacher's wife came to see us off. Pujok tied Joan in the bag to the sled. "Hu-hu," they grunted at the dogs. We were off with a jerk. The dogs fought during the start, and the drivers kicked and rapped them with anything they could find. But by the time we reached the graveyard the five teams, from different parts of the village, had become a single column of seventy trotting dogs.

We had expected the effects of the new low pressure buildup about six o'clock in the morning; we turned out to be right. As we reached the middle of the mountain plateau the wind sprang up from the northwest, with blowing snow along the ground. We pressed on without a pause and passed the first cabin, not daring to stop there lest we become weathered in.

It was a trip that we shall long remember. Sitting up in our sleeping bags on the sled, holding on for dear life, we raced down the steep mountain slopes, across hummocks and driftwood along the beach. The sleds capsized and we fell off time and time again, but the dogs pressed on against the blizzard, and the Eskimos continued to run behind the sleds, mile after mile, with an endurance unique to these people.

At long last we reached the hunting cabin midway between Savoonga and Sevuokok. Here we halted until all the teams arrived. One of the runners on Pujok's sled had broken in the pack ice; this he now mended, standing in the blowing snow, lashing and hammering away, while the rest of us gathered around a stove fire of kindling wood and blubber.

The rest of the journey became a test of endurance. The storm increased; the fierce-blowing snow formed a blinding wall before us and quickly wiped out our tracks. We were completely at the mercy of the Eskimos. They sensed their way across the coast. The teams lost contact and continued separately, westward; we depended on the dogs to find the way. Sitting curled up in the sleeping bag on the bouncing sled was a most uncomfortable ordeal; our buttocks were bruised, our legs numb, and we were chilled to the marrow. At frequent intervals we had to rub our noses with our icy mittens to restore circulation and had to thaw the ice away from our frozen eyelashes. We passed places that appeared strangely familiar as in a nightmare. The Eskimos, with their remarkable stamina, carried on unaffected hour after hour. At least they had the advantage of being able to keep warm by running.

The last stretch was an interminable torture. Thoroughly frozen and bruised from all the insults of the bouncing sled, we struggled simply to keep alive, making faces in order to prevent our noses and cheeks from freezing. Finally, we were down on the lagoon, ice-smooth like a mirror with all the snow blown away by the wind, and the gale so strong that the dogs were swept off their feet. We had reached the northern end of the lagoon when a strong gust carried the dogs and the sled clear back to the opposite end, so now we had to crawl along the edge over a terrible terrain of boulders and almost insurmountable obstacles.

After what seemed an eternity we reached the village. In the kitchen of the church we met the minister, standing like a ghost, staring in silence. It turned out that the girl who we had been told was suffering from acute appendicitis was not too sick to be able to run and hide herself behind a door when we went to examine her.

Our work continued according to schedule. We concluded our experiments with a group of Eskimo women whom we kept for 24-hour periods in the loft of the church in order to control their intake of food and output of urine and stool as part of the procedure required for metabolic studies. Two of them were so attractive that some of the young men struggled all night long in the terrible cold to get into the loft through the small ventilation opening in the roof.

Part of our program consisted in collecting for analysis all the urine produced in twenty-four hours. One day as we were sitting at the table in the kitchen enjoying our lunch, it started to drip from the ceiling, like melted water from the roof, and landed in our soup bowls. In the loft we could hear our subjects giggling and making fun of the girl who had missed the sample bottle.

This was the end. The following day we took off from the ice on the lagoon with all our data, tipped the wings as a last farewell to our friends who had gathered on the beach, and headed across Bering Strait, bound for Fairbanks and the arctic spring.

8 TO THE INLAND ESKIMOS

The spring comes all of a sudden in Fairbanks. On April 1 it is still winter; two days later melt-water starts to trickle through the drainage pipes from the roofs, and a couple of weeks after that the snow is gone. The ground melts all the way down to the permafrost, the streets flood, and large lakes form in the fields. The sun glitters on water everywhere, withered straws protrude through the muck and are mirrored in the ponds. On the slopes facing south the soil steams.

Then suddenly the water soaks into the ground and the mud turns into dust, which is whirled into the air and settles like clouds along the roads. The cats howl in the night, the dogs roam in wild herds. Mating time.

We needed to compare our findings among the coastal Eskimos with similar observations among the inland people at Anaktuvuk Pass in the Brooks Range to the north. These inland Eskimos, the Nunamiuts, were nomadic caribou hunters and lived in primitive skin tents the year round, eating principally caribou meat. The only way to get there before June was to land in an aircraft equipped with skis on a frozen lake in the pass. So we had to take off while there was still snow on the ground at Fairbanks.

It was already bright daylight when the alarm clock went off shortly before 5 A.M. The rising sun shone through the naked trees in the small wood back of our house, turning the trunks and the leafless twigs of the birches into gold. The air was brilliantly clear and crisp. There is something invigorating and enchanting about the arctic spring. "It is worth enduring the winter darkness for the spring," Joan would say.

She had to stay behind this time because of the weight limitations of the small aircraft. I dressed for a major expedition. The jeep pulled up in front of the house. We could clearly hear the cracking sound of the ice on the ponds, which had frozen during the night, crushing under the wheels of the jeep. The melt-water was already trickling from the roof; it dripped down my neck as I went through the door, carrying my baggage out to the car.

We drove to the administration building on the air base. In the weather office we were told that it was clear north of Brooks Range but that there was frost fog in the pass and along the valleys on the southern slope. "On the whole, the prospects are good," said the weather officer. A low-pressure center was moving northward in Bering Strait but was expected to bypass our area. If necessary, we could climb above the overcast and make our approach to the pass from the north. The distance was only 250 miles, and we carried enough gas to take us there and back.

This was the first time a military aircraft was to land in the pass. The bush pilots, however, had been flying in and out for the past fifteen years, as long as the Eskimos had been there. The existence of this inland tribe in the pass had been known to everyone who had been concerned with Eskimo affairs. Scientists had visited them on and off since 1941. Thus we were not about to encounter a newly discovered tribe, and knew quite well what to expect.

We climbed into the Canadian-built "Beaver" aircraft. The pilot started the engine, while the mechanic attempted to free the skis, which had frozen to the ground, but only after we had run the engine up to full power could we jerk ourselves loose.

We passed over clearings in the woods where small homesteads were being hacked out of the wilderness. From then on there was nothing but forest and wilderness, heavy timber and windfallen trees. Here and there we came across a solitary sled track between lonely trappers' cabins. Once in a while we caught sight of a moose as we swooped above the treetops. When we reached the Yukon River we set course due north. Fog had settled along the entire stretch of the river as far as we could see, like an interminable ocean of white wool. Then we once again came out into clear weather, flew across fields of wind-blown snow between the forests and across rivers that wound their way from the mountains down to the Yukon. Ahead of us the peaks of Brooks Range rose above the clouds. By now we had been in the air for an hour. The pilot decided to fly by the compass over the clouds toward Umiat and then to slip into the pass from the north.

We flew over the puffy masses of clouds flanked by mountains on both sides. We were barely able to climb over a peak protruding through the fog like a cone, and below on the flat plateau we could see tracks in the snow and a herd of caribou on the run. The actual mountain range rose some 1,000 feet above us. We started to climb, got across, and found a crack in the undercast. Diving through, we suddenly found ourselves looking down into a frightening world of wild mountains with precipitous cliffs and jagged peaks surrounded by fog on all sides. To the north the mountains gave way on both sides and formed an opening ahead; we assumed that this was the south end of the pass into the tundra. If we were correct, the Eskimo settlement had to be somewhere below us.

Eventually, flying low and following the river, we discovered a sled track and a few moments later we passed over a dog team on its way up the valley. The man sitting on the sled was waving at us. In a clearing in the willows we saw another man sitting in the snow, repairing his snowshoes. As we thundered overhead we scared up flock upon flock of ptarmigan that had been sitting in the willow bushes.

Now we were heading for a large clearing, and there was the snow-covered lake surrounded by steep mountain slopes. We fastened our seat belts, the skis of the aircraft touched the wind-blown snow crust, made a jump, landed, and eventually came to a halt.

"Gee, what a lonely place," said the pilot with a shiver. To me it was like a home-coming; the country reminded me of Greenland and of Norway. I should have liked to spend a week there with a pair of skis, a tent, and a rucksack full of food.

We climbed out and started to walk along the dog trail toward the willows. Suddenly a child appeared over the crest of a hill, a boy perhaps eight years old, dressed in a peaked cap, poplin anorak with colorful trimmings, and a pair of ragged trousers. His face was tanned by the sun, and when he smiled at us he showed his dimples and his perfect teeth.

"Hello!" he shouted happily.

Some distance behind came his father, Mekiana, foster brother of an Eskimo we knew in Kaktovik. He was a sun-tanned sturdy fellow about forty-five years old. He did not say very much, but answered our questions in excellent English.

The mountain rising from the lake is called Anak, which, he explained, merely means a pile of manure. Anaktuvuk means a place where there are plenty of caribou droppings. He went on to say that the pass had from ancient times been an important trail for the caribou herds during their annual migrations toward the tundra in the spring and back toward the forests late in the fall.

"We sit here waiting for them to come. We expect them any day now on their way to the north," he told us. No doubt he was right, for we had seen some of the forerunners of the large herds down in the valley as we flew in.

Mekiana had lived in the pass for the past six years. Originally he came from Barrow but his wife belonged to the inland Eskimos, the Nunamiuts. These nomadic tribes at one time roamed through vast areas of this immense mountain range around the headwaters of the Colville River and to the east as far as into Canada. There they had hunted caribou during winter, moving to the coast every spring. Around the turn of the century starvation forced them to leave the mountains for good and move to the coast. The group that now inhabited the pass moved in from the coast in 1935, and have remained there ever since without any communication with the coast, in contrast to their ancestors.

Our aircraft mechanic acted fidgety and restless as he stood stamping his feet in the snow, listening to what Mekiana had to say. It was much colder in the pass than he had expected and he was afraid he would have trouble starting the engine if we remained there overnight.

We told Mekiana the purpose of our visit and asked if we could take four of the men back with us to Fairbanks for a week to run some tests on them in our laboratory. This was in order, he assured us, without winking an eye. The pilot interrupted to say cautiously that we could not guarantee that we would be able to bring them back until the summer; this did not worry Mekiana in the least.

He liked it in the pass, Mekiana said, but confided that he would prefer to live at the edge of the tree line forty miles farther south, at a place known as Hunts Fork, where the three rivers flowed together, because at Hunts Fork there was plenty of timber. He had recently been appointed postmaster, at a salary of $25 a month, and now if he could only persuade the rest of the Eskimos to move, he would like to build a post office of logs and settle next to the Irish trader who also operated a general store there.

As we stood talking, more Eskimos gathered around us. We selected four of the healthiest-looking men to take back to Fairbanks. The postmaster was one of them, but he said he had to ask his wife first. The rest of them had no reservations. The pilot gave them an hour to get ready.

We followed them back to their camp in the willows, along the beaten path made by the dogs and the sleds. The young hunters trotted along ahead of us with short, bouncing strides, their hands in their pockets. They were remarkably tall and slender in comparison with the usual coastal Eskimo. The children ran about in constant play, throwing snow down the necks of their smaller brothers and sisters, scratching out names in the snow with their long willow sticks, dashing up the steep hard-packed snowbanks to come sliding down on their seats, the echo of their laughter traveling back and forth between the mountains.

The path twisted close to the foot of the moraine hills; there were ptarmigan tracks in the snow everywhere. On the other side of the path the willow brush extended across the valley toward the sheer cliffs and towering peaks of the mountains rising from the flats. The willow brush became denser and taller; a sled track took off to the right, and in a small clearing in the brush we caught a glimpse of the first tent. The dogs were tied beside a sled, a clothesline was stretched between the bushes. The dogs were larger and stronger than the ordinary Alaskan dogs, but even here the Eskimos used screws and iron nails in their sleds, rather than a lashing of skin ropes.

Mekiana had pitched his tent close by the trail in a clearing in the dense willows. We were met by a flock of women and children, representing no more than three families but with all the children quite a crowd, nevertheless. An old woman with gold-rimmed glasses came to greet us, smoking a cigarette stuck in a long silver cigarette holder.

In this circular clearing in the wood the sled and the dogs were closest to the trail. Opposite them was the meat cache. Caribou heads were strewn about in the snow. At the far end of the clearing there was a dome-shaped tent made of untanned caribou hides stretched over a frame of peeled willow twigs, lashed together with skin ropes.

A year-old boy in his undershirt put his head out the doorway, crawled over the doorstep, and rolled into the snow on his bare bottom and remained lying there with his legs in the air. It became apparent that his mother had cut an opening in his trousers between his legs for convenience. We lifted the skin door and climbed over the doorstep into the tent. The floor, covered with willow twigs, was dry and quite clean. In the middle of the tent was a square, homemade, wood-burning stove, and on top a collection of cooking utensils bought through the mail-order catalogue. Only the knives were of genuine Eskimo style, a broad piece of a saw blade attached to a wooden handle. Under the stove we caught a glimpse of a scruffy black cat.

The family slept upon caribou skins on the floor. In the daytime the skins were rolled up and placed along the walls, and on these rolls they were now sitting. Offering us each a wooden box to sit on, they gathered around a large basin filled with boiled caribou meat. Everybody grabbed a piece and proceeded to cut it or to gnaw the meat off the bones; then they cracked the bones with their knives to get at the marrow.

On a wooden box behind the stove we discovered an old-fashioned radio. A bashful young girl was manipulating the knobs in an effort to bring out the jazz, and was smiling to herself. Her brother, who was to accompany us to Fairbanks, was struggling to change his trousers, hiding behind a towel. In an hour the men were ready to leave. Except for their mukluks, all four were dressed in white man's clothing. One had put on a double-breasted blue jacket with fancy fur trimming around the collar. Another wore battle dress with a lieutenant's bars on the shoulders, a captain's double bars on the cap, in addition to a couple of beer bottle caps and a few shiny buttons.

The aircraft could not possibly take off from the rough ice field with all of us on board. We therefore agreed that the pilot should take the Eskimos to Bettles in one haul and then come back for the rest of us. While waiting we attended to everyone who needed medical treatment, and when the returning aircraft roared in over the camp the girls harnessed the dogs and drove us to the lake. When we eventually joined the Eskimos in Bettles all of us squeezed into the plane like sardines in a can, and headed for Fairbanks.

We circled the city at low altitude so that the Eskimos, who had never seen a multistory concrete building before, would be able to take a good look. Then they had the opportunity to ride in a car, but what intrigued them most, apart from the pigs, which they thought would be animals after their own hearts, was the telephone.

By April 11 we had finished our tests and were ready to fly the Eskimos home. Their families had heard the message which we transmitted over the local radio on the "Tundra Topics" program for the natives and were waiting on the lake with their dogs and their women when we arrived.

The postmaster had prepared a lean-to for us, a frame of willow sticks covered by old canvas, and a layer of twigs spread over the floor. While we proceeded with our medical examinations, the four men who had been to Fairbanks briefed the rest of the group on what they had seen. Soon the tent was filled with people sitting on the caribou skins along the walls. Some of them wanted to know what the girls were like out there in that strange world beyond their mountains.

"First there was silk, then there was more silk, but after that it was about the same as here in our valley," one of the men confessed jokingly.

When they asked the postmaster how he liked the white man's food in Fairbanks, he said it was all right but that he missed his caribou meat. And then he helped himself handsomely from the washbasin his wife had filled with boiled back muscles of caribou, eating quickly, and using the knife instead of his teeth to cut off the pieces. He chewed on a few lumps of boiled kidney suet on the side, and finished the meal with enormous quantities of sweet tea. Everyone who came was given something to eat. The Nunamiuts are fond of boiled meat, and as a rule prefer it well cooked. A whole caribou carcass was kept behind the stove to be thawed, together with a trayful of caribou entrails.

We examined everyone who had any medical complaints. Practically all the women had some kind of indigestion, mostly constipation. They piled into the tent, crawled forward in a kneeling position, with their backs to the door, rolled up their skirts and asked us to palpate their abdomens. Judging by their appearance, these people are examples of perfect health. Closer examination reveals, however, that many of them suffer from dyspepsia and various forms of gastrointestinal disorders. Backaches are common among the women, who work hard. They are by no means free of tuberculosis.

The pilot came in and interrupted our consultations to say that it was clouding over the pass. He did not want to stay much longer and, besides, he feared that soon there would not be enough snow left for him to land on skis in Fairbanks. We left behind our rations and some medicine, said good-by, and took off from the ice and flew southward in among the mountains. The ski landing strip at Fairbanks was flooded, and as we landed the left ski caught on a patch of ground where the snow was completely gone. The aircraft veered off to one side, the pilot lost control, and we ended up in the ditch.

9 THE NUNAMIUTS

The results of the experiments that we performed with the four inland Eskimos whom we brought into the laboratory from Anaktuvuk Pass stimulated our interest in further and more exhaustive studies of the Nunamiuts.

In order to carry out a comprehensive research program among this tribe we needed a team of three investigators and several tons of equipment. We decided to transport personnel and the most delicate instruments in the Beaver aircraft equipped with pontoons. The rest of the equipment was to be parachuted from the twin-engine C-47 aircraft. In July we were ready to go.

However, the weather was unfavorable. Four days in a row we reported at the airfield at 5 A.M. but were unable to take off. One low-pressure center after the other moved in from Bering Strait. Finally there was a break between two low-pressure centers and we decided to take a chance. We took off in the Beaver from the river in the afternoon. Joan and the sergeant were to follow on board the C-47 to Bettles a couple of hours later.

We drifted down the river, winding its way like a narrow channel between the trees. An occasional log floating in the middle of the river did not leave us much room to maneuver, and we ran ashore while trying to turn up against the wind. The mechanic had to get out to shove us off. Eventually we refloated, turned the aircraft upstream, fastened our seat belts, and charged ahead at full speed.

The drifting logs rushed by. We rose until the pontoons barely touched the water and made the curve of the river on one float. By now there was only a very short stretch left before the bridge. The pilot pulled back on the controls and we lifted off the water as we entered the last bend in the river before the bridge, banking sharply to the left and barely clearing the treetops. Then we climbed rapidly, passed over Fairbanks, and continued northward.

We flew into a thin mist and a circular rainbow appeared below, gliding along with us through the drizzling rain. Farther north the fog extended all the way to the ground. Here and there we ran into scattered snow flurries, but as we reached the Yukon River the weather improved. Ahead of us we could distinctly see Brooks Range; only the highest summits were hidden in the fog. In front of us lay the John River, to the right of it Wild River. We decided to follow the former. Below us the valley was green with a luxurious vegetation. Numerous streams came rushing down from the mountains and joined the river on both sides. As we continued upstream the valley narrowed into a canyon; on both sides steep grass-covered slopes extended from the river banks to the rock falls, and above them rose precipitous mountain walls, their peaks blanketed in the fog. On the face of the mountain we could see sheep on the rocky shelves.

At the lower part of the valley we looked down on an old

spruce forest with green moss and many streams. Farther up the forest gave way to the willow brush. Then came the tundra with tussocks, ponds and soggy marshes. There we could see blooming cotton plants, moss, algae on the stones around the birds' nests, and saxifrage higher up on the mountain slopes. Here one may expect to encounter grizzly bears, caribou, ground squirrels, loons, ducks or falcons. The river became gradually smaller; soon it was only a stream, and on the hillsides the spruce gave way to heavy brush.

We had expected to find the Eskimos at Hunts Fork, for the pilot had seen three groups of them moving in that direction three weeks earlier, but though we circled the small lake a couple of times we saw no trace of anyone, nor did we detect any signs of camping places. Soon we reached the brush where the Eskimos had had their winter camp among the willows. Ahead of us Anaktuvuk Pass opened into the tundra and there, to our left, west of the little lake on the north side of a small river, we caught sight of the tents, twelve of them altogether.

Apparently the Eskimos had heard us; presumably the wind had carried the roar of the engine ahead of us up the valley. They came running toward the lake where they knew we were going to land. First came the children, who were the fastest runners, some of them wearing their parents' shoes which were far too big for them and made them wobbly. One of them had large holes in his trousers at the knees, another had lost the seat of his pants. Some of them wore parkas with wolfskin trimming around the hood, others had nothing but a sweater. They led the smaller children by the hand as they ran. Then came the women like a school in their long cotton-covered parkas with the bristling fur around the hoods. Some of them carried their children over the belt-line underneath the parkas. The men came last, somewhat more reserved. There was old Morry, long-legged and slim in his blue parka, his old worn mukluks and denims, gray-haired, bearded, with a crooked pipe between his brown teeth. Behind him came old Hugo, sun-tanned and wrinkled, looking more like an Indian than an Eskimo.

Mekiana, who had been out hunting, came stamping down the hillside east of the lake with a weather-bleached cane in his hand, his rifle in a caribou container across his shoulders, and the binoculars in a bag around his neck.

As we flew over the camp along the river we could distinguish the postmaster's tent standing by itself upon the hill high above all the rest of them. It was easily recognizable because of the pink parachute canopy which was stretched over the roof, and the tall radio antenna. The rest of the tents were pitched in the old river bed, on moss-covered fields, or on clearings in the brush. The dogs looked scruffy and unkempt with a molting summer coat, and they were lean because of the shortage of dog feed.

As soon as we landed on the lake we grabbed our belongings and staggered stiff-legged up from the beach in the gray drizzling rain, while the airplane returned to pick up Joan and the sergeant. At this moment the wind shifted to the north. Heavy clouds which had been covering the high mountain peaks came drifting southward, clinging to the sides of the mountains and leaving the valley in the clear.

We started to look for a suitable location for our camp. There were only two possibilities: either here at the shore of the lake below the landbrink, where there was shelter from the wind and only a short distance to go for our supply of water, or next to the Eskimo village by the river. There, for reasons of hygiene, we would have to establish our camp above the Eskimo settlement. However, it was too far to carry all our equipment, so we decided to establish our tent camp by the lake.

Next we had to locate a place where the C-47 could land our equipment by parachute. Fortunately there was a several-mile-long strip of tundra running parallel with the lake a short distance above our camp site. We stretched out the yellow ground sheets which were to serve as markers, unpacked the smoke bombs, and made our signal flares ready.

Then, sitting in the heather by the lake where the mosquitoes were particularly plentiful, we began to take blood samples to be shipped back to our laboratory in Fairbanks. When it started to rain we were forced to retreat under a sheet of canvas with our syringes. Mekiana went down to the beach to bring up some long willow poles which he had used for his meat cache the previous winter. With these we constructed a sort of lean-to, and thus sheltered we proceeded to centrifuge the blood with the aid of a hand centrifuge.

As we were busy turning the crank of the centrifuge the Beaver returned. It came straight in from the south, close above the ground, made a pass north of the lake, lost altitude, lowered the air brakes, and it was evident that the pilot was preparing to land from the north. Apparently he did not realize that the wind had changed since his previous landing and that he now was about to land downwind. We stood there with the smoke bombs in our hands, and held our breath.

The plane came in low over the lake but as we expected the pilot had difficulty bringing it in. Soon they were halfway down the lake but still airborne. Finally the floats touched the water, but the aircraft continued at undiminished speed. Now they were not far from land, and they continued to skip across the surface, the spray gushing about the pontoons.

I was taking a movie of the landing but in my anxiety I dropped the camera and watched in concern as the aircraft came thundering at full speed toward the beach. A moment later it ran ashore. The floats hit the water's edge, the plane made a jump and continued more than four hundred feet inland, skidding across the marshy meadow as if this were normal procedure.

It had hardly come to a halt when the pilot and the mechanic dropped out of the cockpit. The pilot started to run in circles around the airplane like a decapitated cockerel, while the mechanic took pictures with his camera. Out crawled Joan and the sergeant, apparently unaware of the danger they had been in.

It was a miracle that it turned out as it did. It so happened that where they hit land the marshy tundra descended evenly and smoothly to the lake. Had they hit the beach only a few yards west, where the edge rose four feet above the water, they would undoubtedly have made a somersault and probably been killed.

Now the C-47 appeared among the clouds, coming in low with the door open, ready to paradrop. It made a circle over the field, and we lit the smoke bombs to show the pilot the direction of the wind. Then we drove the Eskimo children away. The first package dropped exactly over the marker—two jerry cans filled with kerosene, tied together and attached to a parachute; they hit the ground with a thud that sent the peat flying in all directions. The Eskimos yelled in excitement.

In the same manner there came falling through the air tents, beds, chairs, tables, and numerous utensils, laboratory equipment, sleeping bags, provisions, and all kinds of things that could not be flown in by the small single-engine airplane. We ran across the tundra as the bundles descended, collapsed the chutes before the wind got hold of the canopies, and hauled the bundles back to the camp.

Meanwhile the pilot was shouting for help to pull the Beaver back onto the lake, but we were too busy to pay any attention to him. When we finally took a look we discovered that the Eskimo women had gathered around the plane, lifted it by its wings and turned it around, and now were pushing it straight back into the water with the pilot strapped to his seat in the cockpit. The C-47 was circling overhead to see what would happen. One of the main struts of the port pontoon had been cracked during the impact. However, the pilot was able to take off and both aircraft disappeared southward through the pass.

We sorted out the equipment and erected a temporary shelter from a tarpaulin stretched over a frame of willow poles, then unpacked the rations and invited the postmaster to share our meal. We had appointed him temporary assistant for the fee of one cigar a day.

A ground squirrel had its lair in a hole under a willow. It was sitting there fat and round like a ball, peering at us with its head tilted. A lemming was busy carrying buds and leaves from the willows to its nest under a bush on the hill behind our tent. A duck was feeding among the reeds. As the wind died down, the trout began to leap.

Toward evening the mosquitoes started to swarm. None of us had ever seen so many mosquitoes. They came at us across the tundra like a cloud, avid for human blood. We stamped on them as we walked, and brushed them off our faces by the dozen, only to make room for additional dozens waiting to get at us. The mosquito ointment and the insecticide bombs were packed in one of the boxes that had not yet arrived, so we borrowed a bottle of mosquito repellent from the Eskimos. We brought out some mosquito netting which we wrapped around our heads, to no avail. All we achieved was to trap the blood-filled insects, which continued to gorge themselves at our expense, inside our clothing and in our hair. It was impossible to drive them away.

In the evening the Beaver finally returned with more equipment. The mechanic had made a temporary repair to the damaged pontoon strut. However, the metabolism apparatus and some of the essential items of scientific equipment were still to come.

By this time we had put up a temporary sleeping tent for Joan, with mosquito netting over a folding cot, but we stayed up waiting for the aircraft to return. In the meantime the wind had died down completely. The mosquitoes were worse than ever; the green head nets were now red from blood. Fog drifted southward through the pass. By midnight it filled the valley so that we could not even see across the lake.

Eventually we heard the aircraft overhead but could see nothing through the fog. We could hear it turn around between the mountains farther north, come back, and circle over the lake for quite a while. Then the drone of the engine faded away for good and we went to bed to fight with the mosquitoes in our sleep.

There was still fog over the lake when we woke up; it was warm and moist, the mist was suspended like a veil through which the sun was barely visible, shining through it to form a shadowless overhead light without rays. Everything about us was white without boundaries, without depth or distance, and as silent as in a grave. Once in a while there came a faint bark from a dog, sounding infinitely far away, the echoes bouncing back and forth between the mountains so that it was impossible to determine exactly where it came from.

We remained in uncertainty throughout the day. Large aircraft passed overhead through the pass. A B-52 weather plane roared over the mountains on its way to the North Pole but our little Beaver aircraft failed to appear. We erected another tent to be used as a kitchen and there the sergeant put up his bed.

It started to rain, turning into the kind of nasty mountain weather so typical of the tundra. We walked over to the Eskimos to while away our time.

High up on the hill was the postmaster's tent, constructed in the fashion of their forefathers'. They start with the main beams, long poles which they bend into a curved beam, thrusting both ends into the ground. Then they form the rest of the struts and lash them together with skin ropes. Finally the frame is covered with more than twenty scraped and dried caribou skins, which are eventually tanned by the spiraling smoke from the fire. A window is made from the dried transparent bearded-seal intestines. Two caribou skins tied together serve as a door. The caribou skins may be rolled up near the ground at any point of the dome-shaped wall, thus allowing fresh air to circulate through the igloo. Inside the igloo a large mosquito net, supported by ropes fastened to the roof, encloses the sleeping area. The floor is covered with willow twigs and leaves. As the twigs become too dry or get stamped into the ground they are burned and replaced by fresh ones. Footgear and parkas are hung up under the roof to dry.

In one corner the postmaster had a small desk nailed together from willow twigs with a drawer made of boxwood, supplied with a huge padlock. This served as the post-office counter; on top of it was a homemade wooden box, also equipped with a padlock, containing registered mail. The postmaster carried the key on a string fastened to the button of his shirt.

One day he described the structure of their society and their form of government. "In earlier times there was no chief," he explained. They were governed by the oldest men and the word of the parents was law in the family. However, at the demand of the whites a village council had been established two years earlier. It consisted of eight Eskimo members headed by a chairman. The council is elected yearly.

Wien Alaska Airlines managed to arrange for federal support for regular flights with mail to Anaktuvuk Pass, one flight on the first Sunday in every month. The Irish trader at Hunts Fork wanted to attract the Eskimos there and had managed to enlist the support of the newly appointed postmaster, but one of the council members who had fallen out with the trader mobilized the Eskimos to a general vote to decide the issue. They voted that the post office should remain at Anaktuvuk Pass, and the postmaster had to bow to the majority's wish.

In the meantime the trader had tried to win support for a vote to change the name of Hunts Fork to Anaktuvuk Pass as a countermove. He failed in this attempt, too, since the airline also was interested in seeing that the post office remained in the pass, because they could not land their planes on the tiny lake at Hunts Fork.

The following day was calm with bright sun and the humming of mosquitoes early in the morning. We put up all our tents and established our laboratory. By now we had a cook tent and two sleeping tents, equipped with folding chairs and tables. Later we went outside in the sun under mosquito nets to make medical examinations of the Eskimos.

At noon a small single-engine aircraft equipped with pontoons came through the pass, circled, and landed on the lake. It was Terris Moore, then the president of the University of Alaska. He brought with him a white-haired professor from Harvard. They were looking for a scientist who was roaming among the mountains with one of the Eskimo families. The professor was traveling as a tourist and intended to spend a month living in the Eskimo manner while painting their portraits. He was searching for a paradise with real natives, he explained, and the rumor had reached him in Boston that these Nunamiuts still lived as Stone Age people, that this was a precious prehistoric treasure, untouched by our technology.

We told him that there was a very lively air traffic through the pass. Huge passenger planes and other aircraft thundered daily over the mountains to Barrow and the North Pole. Wien Airlines scurried back and forth with mail and all sorts of merchandise, float planes landed on the lake to unload gasoline and supplies for scientists and engineers in the field; helicopters fluttered about in the mountains and one day three Weasel tractors paraded through the Eskimo camp. They had been in the field looking for oil.

"I thought this was supposed to be a primitive, isolated

tribe," muttered the professor with a sigh, and fastened his seat belt.

In the afternoon the bush pilot arrived from Bettles with the mail and more of our equipment. Now we were alone, the three of us, by the lake, with the postmaster as our faithful assistant.

One rainy day twelve Eskimos arrived from Tuluak Lake for medical examination and to receive our tetanus vaccination. They were the Roland family, the dynamic Elijah and Paneak with a horde of kids. Paneak walked in front, suntanned and erect, dressed in caribou mukluks, denims, and a blanket parka equipped with a zipper, pulled over a heavy black-and-white plaid cotton shirt. He shook hands and greeted everyone in a loud deep voice. Behind the family trotted the pack dogs, loaded with cooking utensils and all kinds of equipment.

At the same time a C-47 appeared over the camp and dropped additional equipment and supplies. No sooner was it out of sight than a helicopter and a float plane passed overhead. The Eskimos barely looked up, the pack dogs wagged their tails, and the caravan of the "Stone Age" people continued across the tundra to their dwellings in the bushes.

Food was getting scarce in the village, since the arrival of the caribou herds was now long overdue, so the young men prepared to go on a sheep hunt. Before they left and to celebrate the arrival of the Tuluak people, the council chairman decided that a drum dance should be held. The old men brought out the large tubs the women used to wash their clothes in, filled them half-full of water, stretched a caribou skin across the top and secured it around the edges with ropes from one of the parachutes. Then they went into the thickets to find suitable branches to use as drumsticks and started to tune the drums while stretching the skin.

This is how simple it is nowadays. In earlier times they

journeyed several hundred miles down the Colville River to the Arctic Ocean to obtain, through barter, the stomach of a walrus which they used as the drum skin, intestines of bearded seal to be used for windows and sealskin to be used as soles for their mukluks. Now they no longer need to go to all this trouble. All they have to do is to write a letter to Barrow, enclose a check, and the desired items will be delivered by plane. Furthermore, they have discovered that they can make just as much noise with a washtub as with a walrus stomach drum, so they can save themselves even the bother of writing the letter.

The dance was to take place in the largest tent in the village. When we got there in the evening a considerable crowd had already arrived. The two drum tubs were placed in the middle of the floor. Behind them, in the front row, the drummers squatted on a roll of caribou skins. Old Morry was tuning his drum. Next to him was Paneak, playing with the drumsticks, then the energetic Elijah, toothless but with keen eyes below bushy eyebrows. The council chairman and a couple of other young hunters were banging away without noticeable interest.

Old Morry started to hum a strange sort of song without words and without meaning to us whites. The people were singing only contemporary songs, explained the postmaster, because only Morry and Hugo still remembered the old ones. Morry sang several verses, then the rest of them joined in while they vaguely marked the beat by banging the sticks against the edge of the washtubs. Then followed the actual refrain—"An-a-ah, ja-hja-jaaa"—then a bang at the end, and it was all over and finished, without any finale. They still showed the same surprising indifference.

They continued to warm up this way for a while, one of them starting, then the rest joining in. Then all of a sudden Elijah jumped forward like a bristling cat and started to dance. His voice was so hoarse when he shouted that it sounded like a foghorn; his legs quivered and his wildly waving arms hit the stovepipe with such force that it flew across the tent and landed by the wall.

At this point old Morry and Hugo took the floor. It was a sight to remember. The tall slender seventy-year-old men suddenly became as flexible and resilient as young, sappy willow twigs in the spring. They bent their bodies, squatted, continuously marking the beat with the right leg, twisting and turning and moving their arms. At times they jumped like a hare or flapped around like a wounded ptarmigan, all the while shouting "Ajungahjeia!" The audience was jubilant, the dancers sniffed and snorted between the acts.

Later in the night they started to dance in couples, the mating dance, and performed some rather erotic and provocative acts. One couple arrived disguised in caribou fur and face masks, and to roaring applause and jubilation they moved about in rhythmic meandering motions performing the caribou mating dance.

The drum song continued until the wee hours of the morning, when the youth set out in pairs to pick blueberries on the tundra. They remained out until sunrise, tearing across the hills, playing hide-and-seek, their piercing shrieks and calls ringing over the mountains. They whispered and panted under bushes. A somewhat retarded bachelor stood by the willow at the river waiting in vain.

One afternoon, nearly a week later, the sheep hunters returned from the mountains, coming down the slope on the east side of the valley. One of them carried a heavy load, and it was obvious that there was a lot of meat in the skin bags that his dogs carried across their backs. The dogs appeared very tired and moved slowly but they carried their curled tails high. A short distance behind came the second hunter with his dogs, and finally the last man came straggling along. He literally dragged his feet and his dogs were equally stiff-legged.

The hunters left the dogs and the meat to the care of the women while they themselves walked straight into their tents. That evening there was dancing to the drums in their honor. They had walked over ten miles that day across tundra and mountains, through icy-cold glacial rivers, along the lakes over pebble stone and marshes. They had been away five days in all.

The first day they had covered more than fifteen miles. They had taken food for a single meal only, half a pound of meat, some sugar and tea, that was all. In their experience the hungry hunter hunts best. They camped on a plain by a brook at the foot of a steep mountain slope where they knew they would find some sheep. They started a fire and cooked the meat, ate, and had some tea. Then they crawled into their skin sleeping bags, unprotected under the open sky.

Before daybreak the next morning they climbed to the top of the mountain and discovered the sheep down below at a salt lick. They were twelve in all. They shot three, the rest of them escaped. Then they rolled and dragged the carcasses down to a brook, skinned the animals and cut up the meat, and carried as much of it as they could back to the camp. The rest they brought down with the help of the pack dogs. That night they ate boiled meat for supper and gave the entrails to the dogs.

The following day they left the dogs tied by the brook, and each man set out to hunt by himself. They carried on this way until they had a dozen rams altogether. Then they loaded some fifty pounds of meat on each of the dogs, packing it in the two caribou skin bags, supported by broad skin ropes across the dogs' backs, that hung down on either side of the dog, and started on their journey home.

Our work schedule continued to go smoothly, with time off for occasional trips in the company of the Eskimos. We studied them in groups of four, having them spend the night in a separate tent in our camp during the three-day periods of the experiments under completely controlled metabolic conditions.

The day started with a very simple ceremony. The sergeant crawled out of bed and ordered all four subjects to line up behind the tent with their urine bottles. At seven o'clock sharp he gave the signal for them to void. The specimen bottles were then carefully handed through an opening in the laboratory tent where Joan stood ready to receive them for analysis. Then the subjects, one by one, were guided into the metabolism tent, where they were weighed and subjected to further experiments. In this way we collected samples and measured and examined their functions in every respect for three successive days. At each meal we appeared with our scale to weigh every bit of food they ate. In the evenings we whiled the time away around the fire by the beach where we talked, fished, and listened to the rippling brook from the mountain, to the mosquitoes humming over the lake where the trout were jumping. On such perfectly peaceful evenings in the mountains one is reminded that nature is not always a struggle, claw against claw or tooth for tooth.

One day when our overhauled airplane returned with reagents and test tubes for certain blood tests, we took the opportunity to fly to Tuluak Lake to vaccinate the rest of the Eskimos there. On the beach where we landed was a young archaeologist who had spent several weeks digging for remnants of an ancient Eskimo culture. He had established himself upon a moraine ridge, which, as he explained, was once the edge of a huge lake. He had found evidence of camp sites all along the edge of that lake. Here and there one could see flat stones on the ground which, according to him, may well have been the remnants of tent rings. On several of the moraine ridges he had come upon comparatively fresh evidence of human habitation in the form of charcoal or an occasional implement or utensil which an Eskimo might have dropped while sitting there waiting for the game to appear, but he had come to the conclusion that there had never been any extensive or permanent settlement there in the pass, the Eskimos having moved from place to place and stayed in one spot for a short period only. As to what kind of people they were, he could not tell from the evidence he had collected.

We continued on to the Eskimo settlement on a delta where the river made a wide curve as it entered the lake. Four families were living there at that time. Sleds and a variety of equipment were scattered around the tents. Paneak's tent was divided into two compartments by a huge log in the middle. At the far end we could see a couple of bunks, a table, a bench, and some folding chairs. We seated ourselves on the log and prepared to inoculate the children. One by one they stepped forward and presented an arm for the needle, and they all walked away smiling as we gave each of them a small piece of candy for comfort.

Paneak was talkative and had a habit of telling tall tales with a completely straight face. He had one he wanted to sell us for a reasonable price; an anecdote about an Eskimo who was a mixture between a man and a raven. At this point we happened to pick up an old magazine which was lying on the table. In it we found the myth of a boy borne by an Indian woman, conceived by a raven. Paneak had simply changed it for our benefit. And then he laughed and perhaps thought to himself that the whites are not so smart after all.

The Anaktuvuk Pass Eskimos had the highest meat diet of all the Alaskan Eskimos we had studied, and their metabolic rate was also higher than that of any other group we had yet studied. Of particular interest was the fact that they had survived in these mountains for more than a decade on a diet extremely low in iodine. As a result many of them developed signs of endemic goiter, which we were able to reverse by giving them iodine. Their forefathers, however, who inhabited this mountain region for generations, had apparently escaped the disease because they journeyed to the coast every summer where they satisfied their iodine requirement by eating fish and sea mammals, both rich in iodine.

On the evening of our last day in the village we set out westward across the plain to hunt for an ancient camp site at the foot of steep Soakpak Mountain, which Paneak had told us about. There was supposed to be a cave in the mountain where people had lived in ancient times. He had found charcoal in the cave, he said, and in front of the opening a barricade of willow twigs. It was actually old Hugo who discovered the place, he told us, and it was absolutely certain that the people who once inhabited the cave were much smaller of stature than Eskimos nowadays.

We asked the postmaster to point out the location of the cave, but he said he had never been there himself, although it was apparently only half an hour's walk from his tent. However, he gave us the directions others had given him: "Walk up to the mountain and follow the face of the cliff northward."

We wondered, as we walked across the tundra, why they had not been there to have a look at the dwellings of their ancestors. "They are only interested in that which has to do with their daily bread," the sergeant concluded. No doubt there was some truth in that statement. Their entire life and all their actions are focused on food. And by food they mean meat, preferably boiled caribou meat. Game is the first thing they look for when they wake in the morning. Through a telescope they scan the mountains, along the rivers and valleys, and the places where there are natural salt licks. And game is the last thing they talk about before they go to sleep at night, and if you say to them, "But suppose the caribou herds move through the pass during the night while you are all asleep?" they will answer with apparent confidence that there will always be more later.

We stamped through the reindeer moss across the plain, forced our way through the willows along the riverbanks, and continued up the incline toward the mountain. At the face of the cliff there was nothing but rock falls. It appeared inconceivable that people would settle in such a wilderness of boulders. However, we searched the entire slope, looked behind every rock and examined every possibility, but found no trace of the legendary ancient settlement.

On top of a grass-covered ridge we saw a stone block which resembled a miniature man. We remembered Paneak's accounts of some strange small creatures they called "mountain men." They were supposed to hide out up here in the mountains, ready to play their tricks on the Eskimos, setting off avalanches to kill them when they were busy skinning sheep in the hills, and hanging around their tents during the night to scare them.

We were standing on an old dried-out river bed among willow brush and weather-bleached caribou craniums, listening to the river rushing through a cleft in the mountain. Then, all of a sudden, there came a roaring echo from the precipice. It was an eagle taking off from a shelf on the cliff, loosening a stone which came whirling down into the abyss. No wonder people who live beneath such cliffs believe in supernatural beings.

10 SUMMER BY BERING STRAIT

It was still summer in Kotzebue on Bering Strait. Cumulus clouds moved with the breeze under the sun. The bluish-green waters of Kotzebue Bay were free of ice, waves washed over the sand dunes and slapped against the beach. Native boats of all kinds were pitching in the wind along the coast. Behind the sandspit lay the lagoon, bluish-black like a mountain lake, surrounded by tundra grass and green scrub. A variety of aircraft were parked along the road from the airfield to the village, float planes rode the waves on the bay. The dogs were asleep in the gravel holes along the beach.

Many of the families had moved out of their winter houses to spend the summer in tents that had been erected between the houses; others had come in from the surrounding villages and lived in a string of tents along the bay. The children were playing outside the village, fishing for tom cod with primitive tackle, using wooden sticks as fishing rods, or were swimming about in the shallow water, fully dressed, thus combining bathing in the sea with a simple clothes wash. A little five-year-old boy was a passive onlooker, standing there sun-tanned and dark-eyed with a genuine smile on his face under the large cap ornamented with his father's union tag.

Two old men were busy digging in the sand by the road on the tundra. They were sifting the sand between their fingers while mumbling to one another. "Digging for gold," explained the doctor.

We set up our laboratory in the hospital as before and struggled to find the same subjects we had examined during our previous visit. At this time they were scattered all over the coast and were reluctant to commit themselves to our rigorous schedule now that it was midsummer and the nights were long and bright.

In the evening the sun sank toward the sea, but did not set behind the low hills in the north. It remained in the sky like a brilliant moon, shedding its glitter on the sea which was rippled by the gentle breeze blowing across the shallow water.

The boat grated on the gravel as we shoved off from the beach. The waves hammered against the flat bottom and the sea splashed in over the side as we surged ahead. The shoreline slid by. Everywhere there were boats hauled up on the beach, and all of them were equipped with fancy outboard motors. They like speed, these Eskimos, and it seems at times as if they value outboard motors more highly than their wives.

It was close to midnight, the sun had reached its lowest point above the hills, shedding its glow on the weather-bleached logs of the cabins and upon the skins stretched out on the walls to dry. It gleamed like a flame in the windows. We sped on into the arctic midsummer night amidst a spectrum of reflected sunlight: the white tops on the waves, the green grassy coastline, the yellow glitter on the bluish sea, the violet-tinted hills in the arctic mirage to the north, rising from the sea to the far-distant mountains, below the glowing sun under golden clouds.

We crossed the bay and made for the Noatak country where Okratsiak had his summer camp. We could see his tents on a patch of grass on a point. A long flat-bottomed boat was anchored by the beach and behind it a beluga whale was floating in the water. Okratsiak had caught it in the bay the previous night; now his wife was butchering it with her broad-bladed Eskimo knife, standing in the water up to her knees.

His parents lived in the larger of the two tents. His father was over seventy years old. One of the walls of the tent was rolled up, and there we could see the old man lying on a folding cot in his long johns, asleep, his bare feet sticking out of the tent, but the mosquitoes did not attempt to touch his toes. A business suit was carefully hung on a clothes hanger from the ceiling. His sixty-year-old wife was vivacious and fit. She scurried around in her tight-fitting denims, busily engaged in boiling maktaq in a huge iron kettle over an open fire. Strips of bearded-seal meat and maktaq were hanging on poles to be dried in the sun. This old couple had lived in Fairbanks for the past two years; the old man had a job on the railroads. However, they had grown tired of it all and had now returned for good to their native village.

"It was tough," she confided in us, "after having been used to living like the whites. But it was difficult to make ends meet in Fairbanks. There we had rent, electricity and food to pay for, not to speak of the telephone. Here all we need is coffee in the morning, some sugar and milk and pancakes for breakfast. The rest we get free from the sea, and freedom, sunshine, and a lovely view in addition. If we only did not have so many mosquitoes." She sighed and scratched herself behind the ear where the mosquitoes were so dense that the skin was barely visible.

The mosquitoes appeared to be as keen to bite an Eskimo as a white person, but did not seem to bother them very much. They brushed them aside, scratched, pulled a rag over their heads or put on some mosquito repellent.

Okratsiak's wife came wading ashore, followed by a long string of children. We joined her on a log of driftwood and talked about maktaq and Eskimo food. It is only the flippers of the beluga that are eaten raw; the rest of the skin is cut in strips, rinsed in fresh water, and hung on the racks to dry. One has to be particular with the drying, for if it is dried too much it becomes tough and impossible to chew. Then it is brought down and boiled in fresh water and dried completely, and stored with blubber oil in barrels or in the dried stomach pokes of beluga or seal.

Finally Okratsiak appeared and joined us on the log. We agreed to go beluga hunting with him in his longboat, which was nothing more than a flat-bottomed trough that his father had built fifteen years before. It was powered by a 14-horse-power outboard motor. Crossing the Kotzebue Sound, we encountered heavy swell. Ahead of us was the horizon above Bering Strait, to northward green foothills extended in a gentle incline toward the low mountain range below the sun. Far out to sea we could distinguish two black spots. These were the first boats to arrive at the rendezvous. As we moved along several other boats came into sight, and they continued to come from all directions, to congregate where shallow and deep water met.

When we arrived at the rendezvous there were nine craft of all kinds: long narrow river boats from Noatak, heavily constructed boats from Kotzebue, and even a few imported light speedboats of fancy design. There was a cabin cruiser and a large fishing boat with a canvas stretched over a wooden frame on the deck which housed an entire Eskimo family. They were in the middle of preparing their supper as we arrived.

We tied up alongside a little boat riding the seas. The swell was quite heavy and it was hard to see because of the glitter of the sun on the sea. An Eskimo boy was lying on his back, his feet hanging over the gunwale, reading a comic strip about rockets to the moon. The rest of them were joking and laughing in the Eskimo manner. From the roof of the cabin cruiser an Eskimo girl kept a constant watch on the sea. After an hour, it started to get chilly, for the wind was cold. A boy in one of the boats was seasick; he stretched out in the bottom of the boat and pulled a sleeping bag over his head.

Okratsiak explained what was about to happen. "The weather is unfavorable," he told us. Ideally it ought to be absolutely calm to enable the hunters to see clearly the movements of the whale below the surface. Now the whales were farther out, but toward midnight they would come in toward the shallow waters for fish. On their way they had to pass the place where we had anchored, and we would see their blows as they came up to breathe. As soon as they had passed, the entire fleet would start the chase and would try to drive them into shallow water where they could be shot.

More than twenty boats had gathered at the anchorage, and it was already past midnight. The Eskimos stood up frequently to scan the sea through their field glasses. Suddenly one of them shouted: "Beluga!" The cry was repeated and passed along from one boat to the other across the entire fleet.

"They have seen them," shouted Okratsiak excitedly, "the beluga school has passed us on the way to the banks!"

The anchors came up, the lines were pulled into the boats, there was a roar of outboard motors, the splash of water as the entire fleet moved on a broad front northward toward the shore. The lightest craft with their powerful motors came first, followed by the heavy smacks. Neatly and in an orderly fashion they fanned out without a word of command to take position in a straight line. We continued this way northward straight into the sun. It sparkled redly on the sea, for the sun was low.

As we approached the coast on the other side of the bay we could see boats coming toward us from the shore. Inside, to our right, was the school of beluga. All we could see of the whales were the blows; we counted about fifty blowing at one time.

At this point the boats approaching each other from opposite directions came together, and now all of them turned toward the shallow water and continued in an uninterrupted single line extending from the northern shore all the way to the sandbanks in the middle of Kotzebue Sound.

We crisscrossed back and forth as the boats moved in formation toward the shallow water, pushing the beluga ahead of us, slowly and with patience. "It is important not to be too eager," explained Okratsiak. "It might make the whales scatter or settle on the bottom."

"We are now in three fathoms of water," said the captain, Okratsiak's father. Up to then he had been asleep in the stern; now he changed places with us and took his position standing in the bow of the boat, measuring the depth of the water with a pole as we advanced. He followed the slightest move of the craft with an experienced eye and gave his instructions to Okratsiak, who also was now standing up. The rest of us had to crouch as low as possible, not to be in their way.

The captain brought out his two harpoons, long poles of driftwood with an iron spike in the end. The harpoon head is so constructed that it turns crosswise inside the whale when the harpooner pulls in the line. He placed one harpoon on each side of the boat, ready for action. Then he brought out two watertight cans to which was attached a 20-foot line, with a sinker tied onto the free end. This was the marker which is used to locate the whale when it is shot. Finally he pulled out the rifle from the canvas container, inserted the cartridges, and put on the safety catch, still searching the sea for signs of the whales.

One of the speed boats had moved too far ahead. The Eskimos shouted and waved to bring it back into line, but it was too late. It had already frightened the whales.

We noticed that the belugas had stopped, the blows appeared at the same spot time and time again; there was no longer any movement in the school. The closest of the whales was only a couple of hundred yards from our boat and we caught a glimpse of its back. It glimmered white in the sun against the bluish-green sea. A moment later it was gone.

Then all became quiet; the boats had stopped. The skippers were standing by to see what might develop, but the whales remained out of sight.

"They have escaped," concluded Okratsiak. "They have probably dived under the boats and moved out to deeper water."

By now the sun was touching the crest of the mountain range in the north and turned the sea into flaming gold. It twinkled and glimmered in yellowish green and red. The banks stood out like a rusty brown line farther in where it was calm without any swell. A faint mist covered the land.

One by one the boats started their outboards to return to the anchorage to wait and to give it another try later. We beached our boat at the summer camp, where Eskimos from up and down the coast had gathered in their tent camps to fish. They had pitched their tents on a sandspit between the sea and the lagoon. Strips of meat and stomachs were hanging from the racks to dry. Next to the racks the large kettles were steaming over the open fires, where they were boiling maktaq and blubber oil.

Most of the people were still asleep in the tents but some of the children were running around among the dogs although it was three o'clock in the morning. The birds were crying out on the lagoon, the arctic poppies swayed in the breeze around the tents.

Okratsiak found his stepsister in the camp, and she decided to accompany us to Kotzebue. While we made some hot cocoa in the boat she pulled down her tent and came dragging her possessions with her, a tent canvas, a suitcase, and a cardboard box kept together with a rope.

We shivered and felt miserably cold the few hours it took to circumnavigate the numerous sandbanks across Kotzebue Sound. We ran aground a couple of times and got soaking wet while trying to get off. The sun was high in the sky when we finally reached Kotzebue.

It was hard for the Eskimos to keep their appointments for our studies. It was summer, after all; the day lasted the full twenty-four hours, and in these midsummer nights there were many temptations. One of the Eskimos had gone berrypicking. Another had a new outboard motor to test. A third had a sweetheart living in a tent nearby and could not very well stay away for long at a time. We traveled up and down the coast trying to persuade them to come to the laboratory, but they all had an excuse. It is not natural for Eskimos to say no, so when possible they hid behind the house until we had left. When it rained, however, they came with us gladly, for it was much drier in our Jamesway hut than in their leaky tents.

At one place up the coast we ran into a half-breed. He was standing by the sea mending his fish net when we arrived. A flock of half-dressed children fled into the torn tent and remained in hiding with their mother who was equally shy. Farther along the coast we found another family. The wife was standing with her arms up to the elbows in the blubber kettle. As we approached she dashed into the hut to wash her hands and appeared in a colorful cotton summer dress, and sat on a log of driftwood to allow us to draw our blood sample, in the middle of a swarm of mosquitoes.

Then came the Fourth of July, THE day in Kotzebue. It started shortly after noon with foot races, and everyone joined in, regardless of age or sex. One of the old contestants stumbled and fell, the rest of the mukluk-shod sprinters simply jumped over him and continued in a cloud of sand. The children participated over and over again in the same race until all of them had received a prize. The old women trotted along for all they were worth while holding a hand over their hearts. A flock of mothers galloped along with their babies on their backs under their parkas.

Then followed the maktaq-eating competition. The contestants chewed maktaq and gulped until tears streamed down their cheeks. Two of the girls cut their fingers with the knife while trying to slice the maktaq in front of their noses, and had to be sent to the hospital for treatment. A pistol-shooting contest was followed by a tug of war and a baby beauty contest. The women paraded past the judges, no less than the U.S. marshal and the Presbyterian minister, carrying their tiny beauties under their parkas. The marshal lifted the edge of the parka, the minister took a look, and then both of them nodded.

In the evening there was a general beauty contest, ending in the crowning of the Kotzebue Eskimo Queen. The judges were selected from tourists who had never seen an Eskimo before. They picked a young girl of mixed blood to be the Eskimo Queen. It all ended with a drum dance in the Community Hall where an ensemble of professional Eskimo dancers performed at the rate of $1 an hour.

Thus ended our summer by Bering Strait.

So far our studies had indicated that the reason the Eskimo gets along better in the Arctic than we do is mainly because he is completely adjusted to the environment, and not because of any unique racial endowment. We had found that his higher metabolic heat production is largely due to the so-called specific dynamic action of his high meat diet, resulting in a greater amount of body heat. This conclusion was based on our findings that the groups who had the highest metabolic rate also had the highest meat diet, and that when these Eskimos were placed on our white man's diet, low in protein, their metabolic rate was reduced to that of our white controls. Furthermore, whites eating a diet containing the same amount of meat as the Eskimo diet showed an increase in metabolic rate similar to that of the Eskimo. That the high metabolic rate of the Eskimo is not due to cold exposure or racial factors is evident from the fact that the metabolic rate was also high in the summer when the climate was warm, and that full-blooded Eskimos serving in the army and leading the barracks life of a soldier had metabolic rates identical to those of our white controls.

11 THE SEAL ISLAND

During previous expeditions to the Arctic I had become interested in a type of finger infection known as the "sealer's finger," which is common among people engaged in arctic sealing. It had been generally assumed that the disease was caused by some infectious agent present in the seal and transmitted to the sealer during the skinning and handling of these animals. However, no such infectious agent had ever been clearly identified, hence the etiology remained unknown. The reason for this was mainly the technical difficulties involved in carrying out systematic bacteriological studies under the primitive field conditions that exist during pelagic sealing in the pack ice.

It therefore occurred to me that it would be worth while to investigate whether sealer's finger occurred among the sealers of the Pribilof Islands in Alaska, where adequate facilities for further studies were available at the biological laboratory in the village of St. Paul. For the purpose of investigating this question I had the privilege of visiting the sealing station during the killing season in 1951. Although I found that sealer's finger is extremely rare among the Pribilof sealers, and discovered only one case of it during my stay, I did, nevertheless, learn a great deal about the Pribilof seal.

I flew from Fairbanks to Anchorage in a military aircraft, and caught the weekly Aleutian Airlines flight out of Anchorage. Our route took us along the Aleutian chain and we had a spectacular view of the gigantic Iliamna volcano, rising like a steaming monster some 9,000 feet through the fog. Black lava smoke puffed from the top, was spread by the moving air, and settled as a horizontal band along the mountains.

Gradually the fog lifted, cracks formed in the woolly blankets of mist, and a green landscape appeared. The fog moved like dabs of ragged cotton wool around rugged mountains, rows of active volcanoes surrounded by drifting clouds. Blue water sparkled in the sun through the rifts in the clouds far below. This was the typical Aleut weather. As the sun rose the weather cleared. We continued to wing our way through restless airlayers toward the world of the fur seal. I was the only passenger, and the pilot was an old acquaintance from previous expeditions along the Alaska coast.

Underneath us the land was sliding by, lake after lake between green plains and brown tundra. Once we flew at low altitude over an abandoned air base. A couple of men were standing on the runway between caved-in bunkers and crumbling buildings. This was all that was left of the thousands of soldiers who were based here during the war.

We continued close above the ground along the coast. I was standing next to the pilot in the cabin. Suddenly he pointed. There just ahead of us by the shore of a lake was a grizzly bear with two cubs. They stopped and raised their heads as we thundered over them, and when the pilot banked the plane we caught a glimpse of a herd of caribou swimming in the middle of the lake.

The bear turned around to take another look at us, then she

started to run, but the cubs remained, sitting on the ground gazing into the air. The mother returned to give them a slug with her paw, and all three of them took off into the hills.

For a while we flew side by side with a wild swan; it was making something like sixty miles an hour. It turned its head to look at us, faltered for a moment, then regained its balance and continued in its lazy flight, as we overtook it and surged ahead.

We passed Cold Bay, and saw the fishing fleet out in the harbor, smacks with dories behind. On land we could see the old house ruins, mounds surrounded by driftwood. There the natives once lived, until they were exterminated by the Russians.

It became stormy, the ocean rolled, broke in white foam against land. Flock upon flock of sea gulls and auklets scurried across the surface of the sea. Steep mountain formations rose like castles out of the ocean. On the beach we could see something move, shapeless brown bodies by the hundreds. They raised their heads, slapped their flippers about and hobbled inland, stumbling over each other. These were the sea lions.

We were flying toward the cold front, which according to the pilot was moving westward at a speed of about forty miles an hour. The clouds squeezed down the mountains, covering the peaks, and soon the entire landscape was obscured by the overcast. We dove to get under it, the wind whistled, rattling in the fuselage and tossing the aircraft violently about. The overcast was now only about a hundred feet above the sea. Then it started to rain: the windshield wipers could barely keep the glass clear. Down below, a killer whale was plowing the seas back and forth outside the straits, waiting for the seals.

We were approaching land and could now begin to distinguish the contours of the rocks. Suddenly we found ourselves in the middle of a narrow fiord with steep mountain slopes on both sides. We barely cleared a ragged cliff on an island in the middle of the fiord. I could see no opening ahead; it looked as if we were heading straight into the mountain. But then, all of a sudden, the pilot tossed the plane around a corner in a 90-degree turn. I thought the left wingtip was going to touch the rock. At the same time he cut the power and we barely cleared the face of the mountain; the wheels were on the ground. When we came to a halt we were at the very end of the short runway, the edge of a landbrink which sloped straight into the sea. We had landed at Dutch Harbor.

This was the place we had heard so much about during the war. It was an important naval base then, and the most easterly point that the Japanese ever bombed. They used carrier-based bombers. The first time they were out of luck and failed to hit any important target. The following day an armada of bombers from several carriers rendezvoused over an island farther west for a second attack. While they were gathering their forces, American fighters intercepted and shot down five of the Japanese aircraft.

In the evening we took a dory, powered by an outboard motor, up to the mouth of the river where the Aleuts had put out their salmon nets, and went ashore at the village, a collection of abandoned houses centered around the Russian church. There was no life to be seen.

We walked along a street that the military had built beside the river. Next to the church was the bar, and next to it was the residence of the U.S. marshal, with the women's prison on the second floor. In front of the marshal's house there was a souvenir shop which actually resembled a general grocery store.

This was once a prosperous town teeming with life. It was founded during Bering's second journey, in the eighteenth century, and became the jumping-off spot for the gold prospectors into Alaska. They arrived here during the winter and remained while awaiting the first boat passage to Nome. Also it was a fueling station for the steamers that sailed northward and a harbor for the sailing vessels and the whalers. Later it became an important base for the cod and herring fisheries. At times more than 10,000 people had lived at Dutch Harbor.

After the town was bombed in June, 1941, the military took over, with gigantic construction projects employing a lot of people. They made good wages and the natives became spoiled. The whales were bombed, as the pilots mistook them for submarines. The herring disappeared completely, and with them the cod disappeared too. Now it was almost a ghost town. The houses were abandoned; people had gone and left the doors open behind them. They were attractive little houses with fences around green gardens with shrubbery and pine trees planted by the Russians two centuries ago. The streets were deserted, for most of the natives were engaged in the sealing industry on the Pribilof Islands.

The following day we took to the air once more, although the pilot was concerned about the weather. We flew in a kind of slalom in among the cliffs, zigzagging between the fog banks in terrific turbulence out over the stormy sea. We passed Bogoslof Island, a solitary volcanic island in Bering Strait, "the disappearing island," as it is called by the Aleuts, who claim that it sinks into the sea from time to time. No one lives there, and no one ever lands on its shore. The sea lions reign uncontested on this desolate rock.

Somewhere in the mist to the north there was a group of islands with burned-out volcanoes in Bering Strait, 225 miles from the nearest shore. They are marked Ostrova Bribylova on the old draft. There are five islands in all: St. Paul is the largest, 15 miles long; St. George is the next largest island; Walrus Island is six nautical miles east of St. Paul; Otter Island is four nautical miles to the south, and finally Sea Lion Rock, close to St. Paul Island.

This archipelago is of volcanic origin and consists of sheer, lava-covered rocks rising steeply from the sea, connected with long sand beaches here and there. Beyond the coastline the ground rises in a gentle incline to a plateau in the interior, with scattered rocks and sandy hills, occasionally the crater of an inactive volcano.

It was not until 1786 that Gerasim Pribilof, the Russian sea-farer, discovered the islands while searching for the summer breeding grounds of the fur seal hordes which passed the Aleutian chain every spring, heading north. When Pribilof landed he found evidence that people had been there not long before him: a copper handle of a sword, a chalk pipe and a fireplace. The owners had left so recently that the metal was not yet rusted and the vegetation had not had time to invade the ashes in the fireplace.

According to the legend, the Aleuts knew about this group of islands long before Pribilof came. The legend of the Archipelago Amiq, which was discovered by the young Igadagiq, had been handed down from father to son from the earliest times.

Igadagiq was the son of the Unimak chieftain Skagnikaq. One day he was out fishing in his bidarka when a southeasterly storm came upon him unexpectedly and blew out to sea. For several days he drifted with wind and weather and came to a group of islands he named Amiq. Here he spent the winter, living off the land. During clear weather in the spring he was able to distinguish the mountain peaks of Unimak Island in the south and decided to try to reach it. He was lucky and reached land in four days. The legend has it that he brought back with him many tails and snouts of the sea otter from the remarkable land he had found.

For a long time the Aleuts sang about Amiq, the mysterious land in the mist far in the north. The Russian fur hunters who settled on the Aleutian chain eventually came to suspect that there might be some truth in this legend, for in the spring they saw a steady stream of fur seal swimming northward, to return in the fall with their pups.

Gerasim Pribilof was convinced that the islands really existed, but it took him a long time to find them. During one of his voyages he spent three weeks drifting about in the fog in Bering Strait, listening to sounds that appeared to come from land, a land which eventually was to be named for him. He felt sure that he was close to the legendary islands, but he was unable to find them in the fog.

Finally, according to the Aleuts, the gods either felt sorry for him or had given up their resistance against him. The fog lifted its curtain and the eastern approaches of an island came into sight. He named it St. George Island after the ship. The hunters were left on the moss-covered island and the ship returned to winter harbor in the Aleutians.

The following year, on St. Peter and St. Paul's Day, June 29, the hunters caught sight of another island above the horizon which they named "Peter and Paul." The islands were uninhabited, but the Russians immediately brought in natives from the Aleutian chain to gather the fur of seal and sea otter. There was no grass on the islands at that time, only moss, solidified lava and stone, and myriads of otter and seal.

As we came out of the mist over St. George Island, the first seal rookery came into sight. Then ahead of us we discovered St. Paul Island with the adjacent Walrus Island and Sea Lion Rock. These are the main islands of the Pribilof group, which is part of Alaska. From the air St. Paul is a flat, green island with numerous points and lagoons. Here and there steep rocks rise out of the sea; elsewhere, white sand strands run uninterruptedly along the coast.

We flew at low altitude over hills covered with a luxuriant flora—green, grass-covered fields, reindeer moss on the treeless summits. The colors were bright and gay in the rich vegetation in this moist summer climate with meadow after meadow of arctic poppies, lupines and saxifrage. We could distinctly see the seals on the beach, and thousands of them swimming about in the water.

We landed on the red gravel runway under a blanket of fog, and tied the aircraft down with rope and a couple of fuel drums. The Fish and Wildlife Service manager was on hand to meet us with his car. He was a tall, fair-haired and sturdy Scandinavian. The manager was, in reality, the ruler of the island. He was the one who made all the decisions, and his word was the law. He spoke slowly in a loud and authoritative voice, and walked with long, decisive strides.

He drove us to the village along the red gravel road winding among fields of yellow poppies. The houses were all alike, and arranged in terraces up a slope, with the Russian Orthodox Church in the middle. The streets were made of red volcanic ash. Around the harbor where the waves washed in over the sandbanks were the factory buildings. Here lived a well-organized society with its own physician, a nurse, and a dentist. Herds of black-and-white cows grazed in the fields near the village, and some of them wandered freely about in the street. Chickens flapped aimlessly up and down the steps between the houses.

This island community is actually run by the officials of the Fish and Wildlife Service with headquarters in the States. The government has the monopoly of all sealing activities on the islands, and the native Aleuts are engaged as their employees. In the past the natives were given all that they needed once a year, at the end of the sealing season in the fall: a complete wardrobe with three pairs of shoes, in addition to wages in proportion to their individual output, plus a bonus. The boat arrived five times a year; the Christmas boat came in November, bringing merchandise from the mail-order companies. Now it is different, complained the whites, with the planes coming in once a week bringing cargo and mail. Under the old system they had two months in which to look forward to the arrival of the boat, and the time seemed to pass more quickly that way.

The airplane has changed the natives too, they said. Now they would prefer to take over the entire business themselves. The government officials have started the slow process of making the Aleuts accustomed to administering their own affairs. One thing after another which they previously were given free they now have to purchase, while at the same time they are given a corresponding salary increase. They buy coal at a rate of about a dollar a bag, but the men prefer to buy outboard motors with the money and leave it to the women to gather whatever coal they can find among the remnants of the military camps.

There was a total of 300 natives on St. Paul. They were originally of Aleut stock, but now they are of mixed blood: Scotsmen, Scandinavians, Russians, and passing sailors all have contributed to their present features.

We decided to devote the sunny afternoon to exploring the island, for sunshine is a rare occurrence on the Pribilofs and never lasts very long. However, it was not a simple matter to obtain permission to do any sightseeing. The officials were fussy about formalities on the islands and, in addition, they had had a lot of trouble with the seals that year. The herds were less numerous and unusually shy, so there was some reluctance to take a chance of our disturbing them.

We dickered with the manager who remained thoughtful and silent for a long while, but he granted us permission to visit the northern point of the island. We bumped along in a rattling old truck, across solidified lava ash, and reached a plateau. From there we could hear the noises from the seal rookeries: the lowing and bellowing of fiercely fighting bulls, the sniffling and snorting from ill-tempered, expelled old males; and the cries of the pups, at times resembling the bleating of lambs or the wailing of babies.

Now we could see the actual seal rookery, closest to us the single bulls, fat and fierce-looking creatures scattered or in small groups, and farther away the main body of seals occupying the rocky slope. The ground was black with seals.

We drove on across the hill crest. A male seal had settled in the tall grass by the side of the road. From a distance he resembled a prehistoric saurian. He crawled across the road, raised his body in the grass, and stretching a long, thin neck, opened his hideous throat and roared like a bull, showing long, sharp teeth. He sputtered through his nose like a furious ox, with visible steam around drooping bristles. Slowly the plastic, shapeless body began to move, then suddenly he came toward us with incredible speed, a few jumps at a time. Abruptly he sat down, waving his hind flippers to cool off in the sun, and started to scratch his fur with the claws of his flippers. He looked very old, although he was a young bull, blackish-brown in color like a brown bear, and when he rolled his black, wild eyes, the fiery red-colored skin fold showed under his eyelids.

At an old abandoned lighthouse we left the car and walked through the heather to the shore. Out here on the rocks the auklets and the puffins had their nests. A blue fox was sleeping in the sun on a flat slab of stone at the foot of the precipice, and as we approached the edge, hundreds of sea gulls, auklets and sea parrots flew out from the shelves in the mountain. We climbed down the ledges to the sea and walked along the beach by the foot of the cliffs, nearly deafened by the cries of thousands of birds, stumbled over stones, and slid in bird droppings. The air vibrated from the flapping of their wings, cries echoed against the cliff. Along the face of the rookery birds were nesting as far as one could see, the sun sparkling in the multicolored feathers.

Farther out on the point were the sea lions. Only a few hundred animals in two breeding colonies were left of the many thousands that had once roamed the island. In 1872 there

were 25,000 of them on St. Paul alone. At that time they occupied most of the northern end of the island. Their habits are
largely the same as those of the fur seals, with whom they
maintain a peaceful coexistence, but their harems are smaller.
As a rule, there are no more than ten to twelve cows for each
bull. The young are born in the middle of June. The sea lions
are shyer than the fur seal, and less is known about their inti-
mate habits because it is so difficult to observe them at close
quarters. The bulls fight with terrific fury. Almost the entire
herd leaves the island in the winter, to return during March-
May, the oldest bull being the first to arrive.

As in the case of the fur seal, there is an enormous difference
in size between the male and female sea lion. The fully developed bulls are said to weigh almost a ton, while the cow
weighs only about 500 to 600 pounds.

The Aleuts used to drive the animals into large flocks, known
as "pods," by sneaking between the sea and the sleeping animals under cover of darkness. Suddenly they would jump to
their feet with fierce shouts and yells, and drive most of the
herd inland. Once cut off from the sea, the animals were easy
to control and were driven straight across the island to the
village. In this way the Aleuts saved themselves the trouble of
hauling the skins and the meat from the breeding grounds to
the village with their dog teams. It took them from five days
to three weeks to cover a distance of fifteen miles, depending
on the weather, because sea lions move rather slowly and could
not be pushed too hard in hot weather without their dying of
heat exhaustion. When finally the roaring and panting hordes
came humping along into the village, the entire population was
ready to receive them with rifles and spears.

As time passed, the number of sea lions dwindled. Toward
the end of the nineteenth century there were so few left that
it was no longer practical to drive them; the animals were
slaughtered on the breeding grounds. At the end the Aleuts

killed only enough to provide the necessary hides for their skin boats.

The seals come to the islands solely to breed and spend the rest of the year out at sea. They migrate as far south as California, the females traveling farther than the males. Most of the old bulls spend the winter south of the Aleutian chain or in the Gulf of Alaska.

Between two of the largest breeding grounds on St. Paul a high cliff rises out of the sea. At the edge of this cliff a biologist from the Biological Laboratory in the village had erected a small observation shack with an unrestricted view over the ocean and the breeding grounds. From this shack he had been watching the seals ever since the first animal landed on the beach early in the spring. Day and night he had remained there with his field glasses, his stopwatch, notebooks and paintbrush. He had attached the brush to a long, bamboo pole, and with this he was able to smear paint on the backs of the animals without getting too close, in order to distinguish individual animals within the herd. He had followed them on their migrations to the south to study their habits. I attached myself to him to watch this remarkable spectacle at close quarters, crawling into the shack through a small opening in the wall, covered by a trap door. Through another opening in the front wall we had an excellent view of the entire breeding ground.

It was a typical Pribilof day; the morning came with fog, a set misty atmosphere with drizzling rain. It warmed up in the course of the forenoon and once in a while we could barely make out the contours of the sun through the mist. The steel-gray ocean rolled in heavy swells, lashing with foamy breakers against the shore. The waves washed over the rocks and the surf broke over the sandy beach between the cliffs; the salty spray drizzled over the grassy slopes rising toward the high ground farther in. It was early in May.

The seals were swimming off the coast, old males that had

spent the winter in the waters around the Aleutian chain. Now they were returning to their traditional breeding grounds, as they had year after year, the oldest of the animals arriving first. They glided through the water effortlessly; almost without motion, they rolled over on their backs to rest at the surface, their flippers crossed on their chests. More seals arrived in steadily increasing numbers. They appeared well nourished and in excellent shape. They snorted and grunted, dove, splashed, and rode with the waves on the restless sea in the fog.

Then the first bull came ashore. He was probably at least twelve years old, and probably weighed close to half a ton. Glistening, bluish-black, and with stiffened bristles, he crawled out of the water and settled on a small rock barely sticking out of the sea, now at low tide. He supported himself on the front flippers, raising his huge body and stretching his neck. The waves engulfed him with each swell. Then he slid back into the water and rode with the surf up onto the sandy beach, and wobbled, fat and lazy, onto the shore and established himself on the flat ground in the center of the breeding area, waving his hind flippers to cool himself.

Soon there were several hundred bulls on the beach. The oldest were in the center, while the younger mature males congregated around them on the sand, in the grass, and on the surrounding rocks. At first the bulls are alone, and lie around without fighting. From the time they arrive until the mating is over they never go out to feed, but remain on the spot, guarding their pieces of ground with furious determination, apparently existing without either food or water for a period of two months, while continuously engaged, after the females arrive, in fierce fighting or vigorous mating.

In June the females start to appear, forced ashore by their pregnant condition, guided by their mating instinct. It is as if the female's sole aim in life is to give birth and to mate; otherwise she is indifferent in all her actions and completely at the mercy of the male. The strongest of the bulls capture the pregnant cows as they crawl out of the sea.

And then the fighting starts. It is a matter of the survival of the fittest, a continuous snapping and slashing, as the bulls throw themselves into the battle. The cows follow their masters willingly, and are brushed together into a heap to form a harem. Each bull strives to gather as large a harem as possible. Apparently it is not the individual cow a male fights for; it is all a matter of grabbing what he can, and the more the better. Thus, a harem may vary in size from one to more than a hundred cows.

The bulls are violent in their actions, guarding their property with vicious force. If a neighboring bull gets too close, he is immediately attacked. With raised head, wide-open throat and flaming eyes, with gleaming teeth and steaming nostrils, the owner charges, roaring with an echo that thunders among the rocks. He curves his neck like a prehistoric beast, jumps straight up on all four flippers so that his entire body flies through the air. Then he lowers his head, his long neck stretched out and weaving like a snake. Like a fighting cock, he strikes at the neck of his opponent, slashes deep cuts in his skin, grabs him with his teeth and shakes him violently. Then both contestants roar and hiss a few times, turn around and gallop back to their respective harems on their short, clumsy flippers.

From time to time the bull wobbles around his harem, pushing the cows into a more compact group. If a cow should happen to be so careless as to try to sneak away, he is there at once, grabbing her by the neck with his teeth and tossing her back. All one sees of her is the light-colored abdomen and the flapping flippers as she sails through the air and lands with a plunge in the middle of the harem. She gets up, perhaps somewhat embarrassed, shakes her pelt, yaps at the neighboring cows, and takes the opportunity to lick the bull about his snout. But she does not try to get away again for a while.

Day after day, as we watched from the shack, more cows arrived and the harems grew in size, till the breeding area extended to the sides and up the slope away from the water. In some places the seals were so concentrated that the harems joined and the cows could to some extent move from one harem to the other. Once in a while a bull made an effort to round up his own. Occasionally a female who drifted into the neighboring harem remained there a couple of days before she returned. As long as she moved slowly and only a short distance at a time, she had a chance of getting away.

The bulls relaxed on the sand or on the rocks, lying on their stomachs or half turned over, often in the strangest positions; at times the hind flippers were pulled in under them and the front flippers were stretched out alongside their bodies, so that they looked something like a huge ball. This may have been to conserve body heat during cold weather. Occasionally they rested on a hip, or stretched out alongside one of the cows. When it was humid and hot, they used their stretched hind flippers like a fan, so that the testes hung in the air. Since the temperature of the testes is lower than that of the rest of the body, it may well be that this characteristic position serves to cool them.

Temperature regulation in these animals is quite inefficient. Having no way of losing heat by sweating, they prefer a moist, cool climate, which is obviously why they come to this foggy island with the wet, clammy weather. Normally, the body temperature of the seal is 37° C., but when they are frightened or forced to move quickly during warm weather the temperature rapidly increases to 42° C. or even 44° C. This they cannot endure; they start to pant, breathing becomes difficult, and they collapse and die of heat exhaustion.

The gestation period is about one year, and from a few hours to several days after the cow has come out of the water she gives birth to her pup. It is all over in less than ten minutes, and the newly born pup pulls the umbilical cord with the placenta after him as he crawls about in the sand. For a day or two the cow shows some evidence of motherly care and affection. During lactation the pup experiences the only caress he will ever know in this world. Otherwise his life is a continuous struggle from his first hour of existence to his death. After a couple of days even the mother loses interest in him. However, she continues to feed him until about six days after the delivery, when she is ready to be mated anew.

The seals were not long disturbed by our presence in the shack; soon they calmed down and continued their activities as before. Once a bull found his way up to us and peered in through the trap door. We saw the gray bristles appearing through the opening, then the large, roving eyeballs with the flaming-red skin folds, the yellow teeth, and the open throat. He leaned his four hundred pounds against the wall, then jogged along and disappeared among the scattered bulls resting in the grass at the edge of the cliff and up along the slope.

We had a good view of the rookery, the black rocks and rugged cliffs from the surf up towards the grass slopes at the foot of the hills. In a tiny cove at the edge of the water a bull used to come in every day from the sea at low tide to settle under a three-foot-high rock, on a ledge barely above water. Every time a cow passed by on her way to the sea, he would grab her. He would struggle and splash with his flippers until he had pushed her into the corner below the rock. In this way he managed to salvage some of the windfalls from the master bulls' harems. Innocent as this business might be, it had an air of illegality about it. If the big bulls up above only had any idea of what was going on at the ledge down below!

This went on every day. One day he struggled a long time with a cow; she was unwilling and stubborn, but with patience apparently nothing is impossible. Now he labored with three of them, this cunning youngster, well concealed from the rest of the seals above, but it was not easy, for the ledge was so narrow that he was continually about to slide into the ocean. In the meantime the sea rose and soon he was submerged in the water up to his neck while struggling to keep the cows in place upon the ledge. The water continued to rise, and finally his illegal harem floated away between his flippers. Swaying from side to side and waving his front flippers, he blew air through his nostrils so furiously that the sea foamed around him, until, haggard and wet, he was forced to surrender in the face of the rising sea. Finally he let himself slide down from the rock to be carried with the undertow out to sea.

Directly below the shack a group of harems consisting of fifteen mating bulls, about six hundred cows, and about the same number of pups occupied a territory bordered by the cliff, where we were, the ocean, a point, and a hillock inland. Beyond the point the breeding ground continued, with thousands of seals, as far as we could see.

The young, mature, nonmating males had gathered in the periphery around the rookery. They were onlookers, waiting for their chance. Once in a while they moved closer to tease the bulls. Farther up the slope there was a flock of young seals, most of them two-year-olds, and a couple who had reached maturity. They had landed there by accident, and now they were waiting for an opportunity to sneak back to the sea.

There was teeming life on the breeding ground before us. The individual bulls had established their harems according to definite, easily recognizable geographical features, such as ledges in the rocks, and blocks of stones. The largest, strongest and most ambitious bulls were in the center. Others were out on ledges by the sea. One of them, with a small harem, held an area only a few yards square. On the uneven terrain it was awkward for him to get into position during the mating. He struggled for hours, and the poor cow, squashed flat on the rock with her hind flippers in the air, was impatiently biting the bull's pelt in despair.

In other harems the bulls got up about every ten minutes to make their rounds, sniffing at the nose of each of their cows. At this early stage of the mating game the male was particularly eager, watching his cows with intense interest. He did not lose sight of a single one of them during the period when they might be in heat. As soon as he sensed a possibility, he was there with his snout; if she was ready, she raised her pelvis; otherwise she withdrew her hind flippers and the bull continued on his rounds.

When the bull made a positive finding he would open his mouth wide, shake his head back and forth, and rub the cow along her neck with his cheek. Then he would sit down on his hind flippers, still shaking his head. If he took too long about it, the cow would start to dance around him, nipping impatiently. All this created new excitement in the flock, and the rest of the females would begin to stir and nab at each other.

The bull shoves the cow over on a level piece of ground and she settles flat in the sand. As the monster slides over her she disappears almost completely under the mountain of meat and blubber, five to eight times her own size. All that is now visible are her head with the rolling eyeballs and her hind flippers slapping about the belly of the bull, who looks around with half-open mouth and once in a while barks at a neighbor. The cows gather round and some of the pups crawl up on the bull's back. The rest of the pups run back and forth, bewildered, crying, waving their flippers about, slapping them against the rock, and stumbling over their long hind flippers. The cows low and yap at each other, and the roar of the bulls booms among the cliffs.

After six to eight minutes he wobbles away, turning his back to the cow without so much as giving her a look. He then continues his sniffing rounds, and finally settles in the sand waving his flippers in the air. The cow, on the other hand, remains where he left her, rolling her head back and forth for a while. In this manner the bull may carry on almost indefinitely and may service as many as six cows in four hours.

A day or two after the mating, the cow leaves the harem to feed at sea. She is given free passage to the beach and sets off from the coast. By this time eight to ten days have passed since she gave birth to her pup.

As she heads straight for the sea she appears to be in no hurry, and often several cows join her on her way to the shore. They sit for a while on the slippery, seaweed-covered rocks at the edge of the water before diving in. She turns to look back; the pup is asleep in the sand with a full stomach. Then she leans forward, lowers her head, pushes off with the rear flippers and dives in a curve through the air and glides like a light streak through the surface and disappears. She surfaces a distance away, twists as she shoots her body halfway out of the water, allows herself to sink backward and remains floating on her back while she scratches her skin with her claws and waves her flippers in the air. Then she starts to swim; like a slippery arrow she shoots effortlessly through the water, surging ahead with the hind flippers stretched out and practically motionless, driving herself forward with strokes of the front flippers as if they were the wings of a bird. At each stroke she shoots ahead, and all we can see is her wake in the gray, icy water. She may roam as far as 150 miles offshore, and may stay away as long as five days.

She came swimming with noiseless strokes, diving and turning through the waves, slowing down as she glided by a submerged rock where three bulls were busy barking at each other. Then she slid in toward the beach; without stopping she sneaked out of the sea, stretched her neck to look around, raised herself with the aid of her flippers, and remained upright for a moment. She had looked scruffy and brown when she went out to sea; now she was blackish-gray and shiny with smooth hair, her pelt almost blue.

Then she crawled up over the stones, stopped from time to time, looking around, lowed like a cow, sniffed at all the pups she passed. They clung to her, jumped up on her, sniffed at her face and her udders. Soon there was a long column of pups following her, but she wanted nothing to do with them; they did not belong to her. She shook them off, snapped at those who were closest, and continued on her way. They followed her a while longer, then gave up.

She wandered from stone to stone, smelling, lowing, looking around. The rest of the cows gave her a hard time. Occasionally a bull acted as if he were about to grab her, but then for some reason he would leave her alone. Finally, as if by chance, she was united with her own pup. He had been busy playing in a dirty mudhole, wading in and out, splashing about, sliding into the hole and crawling out again. She settled down in a cleft in the rock with her front flippers hanging over the edge. The pup settled to suckle in her lap, and there they remained for a long while. The mother opened an eye occasionally and raised her snout to take a deep breath that sounded like a sigh. She remained with the pup a day or so before returning to the sea to feed again.

As long as the pup is young the mother keeps him under control. I saw a cow drive away the newborn pup of another cow, so newly born that he still had the cord and the placenta attached. The pup's mother charged immediately, but the bull intervened. The mother grabbed the pup by his hind flippers, but he slipped out of her grip; then she grasped him by the neck, pulled him away, and settled down to feed him. Once we saw the two cows fight over a newly born pup. One pulled on the hind flippers, the other pulled on his neck. In the end the mother won.

The young, fully developed but not pregnant females arrive at the breeding grounds later than the rest of the herd, after the pups are born. They join a harem and are serviced with the rest.

The one-year-old seals arrive at the very end of the migration. No one knows exactly where they spend the summer, but one occasionally comes across a few of them in the waters around the islands. They arrive on the beaches during August, September and October.

The young, not yet mature males continue to come in a steady stream all summer long; they are the ones killed by the sealers. Each sealing field is harvested once every fifth day, to give the young seals time to congregate on the beaches after each catch. Thus the herd is protected to some extent because many of the young seals always escape the sealers, and all that arrive after the end of the sealing season are spared. It is figured that at least 4,000 young males are left at the end of each season, and this is apparently more than enough to satisfy the need on the breeding grounds.

On the day of the first seal drive I witnessed, one of the biologists came to knock on my door two hours after midnight. I jumped into my clothes and ran down the stairs of the guest house where I was staying; the rest of the group that was to participate in the kill was waiting in the hall. It was a gray, misty and dark night. Men dressed in blue jeans and suits of oilskin hurried by. I heard the stamping of heavy boots and the slamming of doors. The Aleut crew was having breakfast in the large dining room, tough pancakes and black coffee. When they finished they filed into the trucks and the convoy started to move. Our little group of observers followed; we drove past the graveyard in the twilight and headed north.

About four dozen men in all participated in the catch. They were dispatched in small groups down to the sea on both sides of the main breeding ground where the harems were located.

Encircling the breeding animals—the large bulls with their harems—were the young "bachelors," and farther out on the beach, outside the rookery, were thousands of younger seals of both sexes. They poured up the beach in a steady stream, putting their heads out of the waves and crawling ashore to sleep.

I walked down to the beach; the roar of the breakers and the cries of the seals rose and fell with the breeze. Here I met the Aleuts in the mist. Like shepherds with their long canes, they came toward me up the grassy slope, driving the seal herd in front of them; the moisture steaming from the animals' throats engulfed them in a blanket of fog. The seals huddled together in flocks; an occasional stray, large bull became mixed up with the young seals that were to be killed. In the mist it looked like a meandering mass of shivering blubber. The herd roared, steamed and snorted; hum-iti-dump, hum-iti-dump, they came jumping on their flippers up the slope. Driven in from different parts of the beach, they were eventually gathered in a single flock numbering a couple of thousand, then chivvied ahead in line on a wide front and ushered onto a flat field by the road. It all happened automatically without much talk or fuss.

The drive over, the animals were left to cool off, with the young boys on guard, while the sealers went back to the trucks for a smoke. A few of the seals died from the heat. Supporting themselves on their flippers and panting with gaping mouths, they collapsed and died almost unnoticed.

The boys played with the seals, crawled toward them trying to copy their movements, teased them with their canes, and seemed to enjoy it when the badgered, fuming bulls charged. It was no joke, really, to tease these raging animals. Maddened by anger, they leaped ahead at terrific speed. At times they would sneak up on the boys from the rear, get hold of their trousers or their boots and bite through to the skin. Occasionally some of them went completely berserk. They would charge into a group of sealers and nothing could stop them; the men had to keep leaping aside until the animal was exhausted.

The slaughtering is admittedly cruel, and yet one does not, perhaps, have the same pity for these animals as one does for the arctic hair seal, which has such an innocent appearance as it looks at its killer with its large, brown, foggy eyes. The Alaskan fur seals, in contrast, are quite hideous. With their pointed ears rolled together into a peaked horn on an unreasonably large, shapeless head, even the seal pups lack the usual innocent charm of newly born creatures. They exist in a world of battle. When only an hour old, they will attack anything that crosses their paths, and they are attacked by all except their own mothers.

The trappers go ruthlessly about their business. With the aid of six-foot-long clubs, they single out a group of twenty to thirty animals which they separate from the rest of the herd. Then they pick out the old bulls who have been included by accident, and drive them away by rattling a tin can at the end of a pole, and let them escape while holding the young seals back. In this way they sort out the animals until only three- to four-year-old males remain in the herd. The fully mature female are practically of the same size as the young males, but they have a more pointed snout, a lighter patch on the chest, and lighter bristles.

As the young bulls come within reach, the sealers club them on the skull, and that is the end. The rejected animals, the old bulls and the females, flee toward the sea. Occasionally they rest on the way, but even now, when they are all faced with a common foe, they continuously fight among themselves.

The seal carcasses are hauled aside and lined up in rows, with ten animals in each row; then a team of butchers goes to work opening the chest. Ten skinners follow, stumping ahead side by side in a straight line, cutting out the skin around the flippers, all around the head, and, finally, making a long slash along the chest. Then comes a team of nine men who pull off the skin. They are divided into three groups, each equipped with one long fork and a hook. The hook is fastened at the edge of the pelt near the neck. One man forces the head to the ground with his fork, while the other two men haul on the hooks, and thus the skin, including the subcutaneous blubber, is pulled off the seal. It is done in a matter of seconds.

One man goes along and measures the length of the seal to assess its approximate age. Behind him follows the supervisor with a pad and pencil. Then comes a team of biologists to cut the tags or bands from the flippers and to collect the testes, which are sold to the Chinese in San Francisco for ten cents apiece. I am told the Chinese eat the minced testes to increase their virility. Some of the biologists collect the livers, others collect the skulls and the teeth for more accurate age determination.

Behind them on the ground are the carcasses, arranged in orderly rows. The pelts are thrown to one side. A couple of men with hay forks shove the carcasses into two rows. A truck pulls ahead to collect the pelts and takes them to the factory. The carcasses are tossed onto a second truck and taken to the by-product factory.

It is all done very smoothly and efficiently, without pause. The crew can handle eight hundred seals in an hour when it operates at full speed.

"Ready for the next lot!" shouts the foreman. Two men sort out the next batch, drive the animals toward the butchers, and the process is repeated.

A swarm of sea gulls were hanging like vultures in the air. They followed in the wake of the crew to clean up anything left behind. A blue fox pricked his pointed ears out of his hole in the ground. He could afford to wait until the men moved on, for he knew from experience that there would be plenty left over for him too.

The animals rejected for conservation purposes—the bulls over four years old and all the females—struggled to find their way back to the sea. Somehow they seemed to know which direction to take. Eventually they approached the seal rookery, where they gathered on the outskirts, on the crest of the hill and the upper part of the slope, a safe distance away from the rutting bulls and their harems. Time and time again they made an attempt to find an opening, waiting for a chance to break through the breeding ground to the sea and its abundant food, but this sometimes took several days.

While I watched one day three young bulls approached the harems; one of them was almost old enough to have a harem of his own. Though driven back viciously, he tried again and charged between two huge bulls. He spun around in circles, received a couple of deep slashes in the neck, rushed back and settled down to sleep.

The smallest of the three bulls became entangled in a harem. The cows sniffed and nabbed at him until, bewildered and frightened, he limped away. He was almost at the edge of the cliff when one of the big bulls surged ahead like a clumsy projectile, grabbed him by the neck, and tossed him high into the air. The smaller bull landed in a cleft at the edge of the precipice, lay flat on the ground for a few moments wiggling his bristles, then came crawling back. The big bull, who had been rushing back and forth, suddenly dove upon the intruder again, sank his teeth into his neck, and sent him flying into the air. Pieces of skin and patches of hair flew in all directions. The young seal swirled in the air, plunged down the 20-foot cliff and landed with a thud on a flat rock in the middle of another harem, where an even bigger bull was ready to receive him. Confused and almost unconscious from the fall, he zigzagged across the slippery stones, over the seaweed, out over the beach, and slid into the sea.

The third young bull was still on the hill behind the rookery, moving restlessly back and forth along the crest, waiting for a chance to break through. Several times he seemed just about to have made up his mind to make a dash, when his courage failed him. Suddenly I saw a clod of sand and there like a bullet he came shooting down the slope, landing between two harems where two furious bulls awaited him. A couple of snaps, and the poor seal, his courage failing him, dashed back up the hill, and settled down to rest in the grass.

In the afternoon I walked along the salty lagoons to the factory where the pelts were prepared. The skins were brought in on trucks, counted, and soaked in brine. From the factory they were taken to a large hall where the blubber was removed with a blunt knife. Next, in an adjacent room, the pelts were stirred in a salt solution for several hours. Following this, the water was squeezed out of the skins in a tobacco-leaf press and the skins were then sorted into large piles. Later they were rolled into bundles, salted and packed into barrels, and shipped to the States to be tanned.

In earlier times there was a tremendous amount of waste in the sealing, and both males and females were slaughtered indiscriminately. In the half century between 1786 and 1834 close to two millions seals were killed, causing a marked decline in the herd. During the years from 1835 to 1867 the females were protected and the herd increased in number. When the United States purchased Alaska in 1867, it was estimated that there were between two and five million seals on the islands.

During the pelagic sealing, a large number of females were killed, with the result that unborn and newly born pups also succumbed. In 1911 a treaty was agreed upon between the United States, Great Britain, Russia and Japan to bring the sealing under strict control. The following year all killing of seals was prohibited by law for fear they would be exterminated. At the same time research was initiated in order to learn more about the biology of the seals, and records were kept of the number of newborn seals. Since then the seals have increased steadily in number.

One afternoon we drove to the south end of the island to study the sea lions. From a hill we looked down on the seal rookery, which extended continuously like a huge anthill all the way around the point. Far out on a stony promontory some sea lions—light, yellowish-brown shapeless monsters—had settled in apparent harmony with the seals. They may possibly push the seals back a little, but otherwise cause them no harm. According to the biologists, however, they do a great deal of damage to the fish stock.

We walked across the plains toward the point where the sea lions were. The seals barely moved out of our way, snorting and showing their teeth and packing closer together. Some of the bulls were quite aggressive; they did not yield an inch, and created such a fierce commotion that we were almost afraid to walk among them.

The sea lions were asleep. Once in a while they lifted their heads and an occasional animal would slide into the water; others crawled out of the sea to settle on the rocks. The pups played on the slippery stones, splashed in the breakers, and huddled together on rocks that projected above the surface.

One huge sea lion had settled down among the seals far inland. The biologist decided to kill it for examination. He took careful aim and fired, and missed. Suddenly, with a deafening roar, the entire anthill went into action. The sea lion with its ton of blubber humped along faster than the rest; he actually galloped on his flippers, booming like rolling thunder. I got out of the way as fast as I could. My biologist friend fired again when the sea lion was close to the water. A shock wave traveled through the mountain of meat, and he sank lifeless among the stones. The sea was colored red around him as the waves washed in over the beach.

The seals fled everywhere; the bulls struggled furiously to keep their harems intact, the bachelors on the periphery became entangled in the harems during the chaos that followed, and fierce fighting broke out. Even the pups joined in, biting at anything they could get hold of and even attacking each other. A terrible uproar developed out on the point where the sea lions had been peacefully asleep. The old bulls dove with a splash from a 15-foot cliff into the sea; the others stormed after them, the water foaming around their huge bodies, and everywhere we could see the small, bluish-black pups popping their necks above the crests of the waves.

One afternoon, late in the summer, I went with the biologist to the observation shack to take my customary look at the seals. It was still the same kind of moist, raw weather: there was a drizzle in the air; veils of fog moved around the rocky cliffs; again and again the sun seemed about to break through, but never quite made it.

It was late in the mating season now and the seals were more restless. The bulls were getting tired; they looked narrow through the pelvis and their ribs were visible beneath the loose skin. The young bulls had become fresh and courageous; they ventured to move in closer to the harems and realized perhaps that each day their chances were increasing. Young, fully matured cows were still arriving on the breeding grounds, and the bull under the cliff at the water's edge was still trying to catch them.

Now the animals were anxious to get out of our way as we approached. The breeding colony had spread out considerably and the harems were gradually becoming more scattered. The pups roamed over a large territory, on the beach and up along the slope. The cows continued to come and go. It was low tide when we arrived; soon the sea would start to rise. Seaweed was drifting toward the land. The sea was packed with seals floating on their backs, waving their flippers in the air.

I sat down in the grass at the edge of the cliff. From there I could survey all the harems simultaneously. The mating was still in full swing. The old bull up on the ledge was active behind a large boulder. I could only see his head and neck.

Down in a cleft in the rock at the edge of the water I noticed three seals pups playing. They slid into the water, crawled back up on the slippery rock, shook the water off their pelts, and started all over again. A large wave washed one of them out to sea. It started hectically to crawl with its front flippers, like a child learning to swim, but got nowhere, and looked around, uncertain and helpless. Suddenly it turned around and moved with the current out among the rocks, swam in a large circle and landed on the beach, a stone's throw away. As it approached the shore, a cow caught sight of it and shot through the water to help. Mostly, however, the adult seals appeared to be quite indifferent to the pups, which were left to play on their own down by the beach.

The other two pups remained for some time at the edge of the rock staring down into the sea; then they looked at each other, and suddenly plunged into the water and swam through an inlet between the rocks to land farther in. They kept this up hour after hour, and other pups joined them. Soon they were all splashing around in the water the length of the beach. They fought a bit, climbed on each other's backs, and nabbed each other in the neck. The bulls stepped on them as they charged around trying to keep the cows together. Soon the pups learned to dodge every time a bull started to move.

Two of the scientists arrived with a long bamboo pole to search for a cow they had marked earlier. They went so close and made so much noise that they created panic in the breeding colony. The cows fled into the sea, and before the bulls could do anything about it they were left with only a couple of females in their harems. The sea became alive with seals shooting back and forth, diving, splashing and snorting. Flock upon flock of migratory birds trekked by close above the surface of the sea, heading south.

After about three months the mating season drew to an end. The bulls moved up the slope to rest a couple of days before they left. The cows came and went for a while longer, but soon they too disappeared. The pups were the last to leave the islands.

12 KUNUK

Our Eskimo studies included a comparison of their physiological functions during winter and summer in order to determine seasonal variations and to single out factors that could be attributed to the effects of cold. It was therefore necessary for us to repeat our studies twice in each of the Eskimo villages we had selected, once during the cold weather and once during the arctic summer.

It was late summer when we returned to St. Lawrence Island in Bering Strait, landing on the lagoon at Sevuokok in a Catalina flying boat. The Eskimos were all there on the beach to meet us, the women with their children on their backs, the men dressed in sealskin trousers and bird-skin parkas with a rim of fur around the edge of the hoods.

They all joined us as we walked across the plains to the village by the sea, a cluster of houses which we could see as silhouettes against the horizon below a thin band of smoke. Behind us the mountain rose like a wall under the cumulus clouds with boulders of rocks and bird rookeries out toward the ocean.

Around the village the breakers rolled relentlessly against the shore. Above the roar of water came the cries of myriad sea birds flying across the sun that was now sinking into the sea, shedding its glitter on the waves. To westward the Siberian coast stood like a shadow on the horizon.

"The youth is working at the south end of the island," explained the talented Kunuk, our faithful assistant from previous visits. "There are mostly women, children and the aged left."

He himself was reluctant to leave his wife to go to work, preferring, he told us, to spend his time carving walrus tusks and make his living that way.

He looked shy and awkward as he walked along with his hands in his pockets, smiling as a matter of habit. He was a young man but he looked frail, and had aged in the months since we had seen him. His wife had had twins not long ago, but one of them died. "It was too much with two at one time," he said.

We passed old abandoned igloos, half underground, with walls of stone and peat, and whale bones to support the roof. This was where the Eskimos from the village now emptied their pots. An old woman was digging in a huge mound of bones for old utensils and artifacts which she would sell to the tourists.

We picked up a piece of bone which resembled a walrus tusk and showed it to Kunuk. The Eskimos giggled when he said, "They have a special name for this around here; it is not a rib, nor is it a femur, but it is good bone all right, for it is the bone which supports the male sex organ of the walrus."

The old man, Tingmiak, captain of the skin boat in which we had gone walrus hunting in March, walked beside us. It was he who had shot the whale this summer.

"I saw the whale at the surface between the ice," he explained. "We approached him in a wide curve, from the side. From a distance of a few yards we thrust the harpoon in his back. He went down with three seal floats attached, and surfaced again a short distance away. We started the outboard and chased him and managed to place a bomb in him with the whale gun. That finished him off. The rest of the boats . joined us to tow him ashore.

"The old village was on the slope under the mountain," Tingmiak continued. "There the people used to have their igloos." He pointed toward the steep, rocky cliff where the sun gleamed on weather-bleached, wooden coffins among the boulders where the Eskimos had buried their dead. This settlement was so old that even his grandmother, who was the oldest Eskimo in the village at the time of her death, never had heard of this site, which had been uncovered by some archaeologists from the University of Alaska. She had told him that in her time there were so many fur seals along the beach that the hunters occasionally were unable to get out of their kayaks because they would be attacked by the furious rutting bulls.

Tingmiak pointed out some tall whale bones sticking up from the gravel by the sea. These, again according to his grandmother, had been used to support a platform on top of which the Sevuokok people took position with their spears and harpoons to defend themselves against the Siberian Eskimos when they arrived in their skin boats to wage war. The Sevuokok Eskimos wore cuirasses made of walrus skin, and trained daily for defense. Every morning they would climb up on the mountain to scan the horizon for signs of the enemy.

Tingmiak was now fairly launched and went on to describe present-day whaling procedure on the island.

The boats set out early in the morning as soon as the crew is awake. "Those who are out at sea first have the greatest chance," he said with a smile. They scout about in their outboard motor-powered whaleboats looking for the spouting of whales who at that time of year are often found playing just underneath the surface. They surface to blow, then dive again, but remain as a rule in the same spot.

As soon as a boat crew has sighted a whale, they hoist the blue flag at the stern, which is the signal to stop all motors and to use only sails in order not to frighten the whale.

The whale gun is made ready, and when the men are within range they fire the harpoon, which is attached to the end of a skin rope. The other end is fastened to a couple of seal floats which serve to prevent the whale from diving too deep. One man stands ready with the rope coil to throw it overboard the moment the shot is fired. This may be a dangerous job; it has happened that the rope has become entangled in the boat and pulled the man overboard. Immediately the harpoon head enters the whale the charge is detonated automatically and the harpoon is thrust deep into his body. As a rule, the whale dives quietly when he is hit, but sometimes he goes berserk. As soon as the harpoon has taken hold, the entire whaling fleet crank up their motors to start the chase. Every time the whale surfaces to breathe, they bombard him with small bombs until he is killed.

In the yard between two weather-bleached houses an old man was completing the wooden frame of an umiak. Now a group of men joined him, hauling two walrus skins, which they stretched over the frame and cut so that they fitted precisely. Then the women took over. They arrived with bundles of sinews, sailmaker's needles, and thimbles, and started to join the two skins with a double seam at the middle of the boat, greasing the sinew at intervals with a chunk of blubber. They worked with amazing skill and speed, and then it was the men's turn again. They pulled the skins off the frame, carried them to the beach to soak them in the sea. Finally they stretched the skins back over the frame and fastened them to the gunwales with skin ropes, and the umiak was ready for use.

"The youngsters nowadays are not interested in making boats," said the old man; "all they care about are radios and motorbikes."

The western sky was glowing red over Siberia, where the sun was setting. The moon appeared from behind the mountain, shedding a band of light on the lagoon. The sound of chiming bells rang through the village; it was ten o'clock, time for all children and unmarried women to be barred indoors, in some sort of curfew imposed by the ruling elders.

"However, it is now that life really starts," explained Kunuk. Earlier in the evening the young men had been around to make their dates and arrangements for the night. One could see them trotting in and out between the houses, their parkas flopping about them as they rounded the corners. About two or three o'clock in the morning, they showed up for their dates, and we saw a girl signaling with a flashlight from her window that the road was clear. This was their fun, and it was all free. After all, there were no other means of entertainment. Even the drum dance was prohibited by the minister.

In the morning we accompanied Kunuk, who was heading for the mountain to catch birds. He had a bag slung across his shoulder, and under his arm he carried a couple of long poles with sharp hooks in the ends.

Eskimo women were collecting edible plants out on the tundra. "There are several kinds of plants which we eat, including the root and stem," explained Kunuk. "They are gathered during the summer, preferably in July, and are prepared for winter food. We also eat all kinds of seaweed, either raw or dipped in boiling water.

"It is the women's job to gather plants. They usually pick only one kind at a time, because the different kinds of plants are treated separately, and certain plants go with certain foods. We put the plants in layers between meat and blubber, and eat this like a sandwich.

"At certain festivals or celebrations we prepare ice cream from the plants according to an old Eskimo recipe. I am always glad to help my wife with this," he said jokingly. "We grind the plants in a mortar of stone, mix them thoroughly with oil from seal or walrus, and whip the whole mixture in a vessel. Then we place it in the snow to freeze. This we eat as a dessert." He was visibly excited by the thought of the delicacy. "The best ice cream is made from trout or salmon roe," he added. "The roe is ground with stones and whipped with blubber oil. Then we freeze it and eat it with our fingers."

We crossed the tundra and came to the sea, followed the coast until we reached the mountain rising in steep cliffs from the sea. We could hear the whistling of wings above us in the mist, the cries of the birds sounded over the roar of the breakers. Out toward the point above the ocean there were birds on every boulder as far as one could see, mostly auklets and puffins. Swarms of birds came sailing down over the piles of rocks to catch fry in the breakers, then flew back up to the rookery with the fish in their beaks, resting for a moment on a boulder before disappearing in cracks between the stones.

We started to climb up the rocky slope, scaring up birds with every step. They shot out of small openings in the ground, dove from the cliff, and fluttered away.

Kunuk crawled in among the huge blocks of stone, knelt down and maneuvered the pole in through a hole. He poked it about, then jerked it and pulled out a tiny nestling, hooked at the end of the pole. The bird looked startled, blinked its eyes in the sudden brightness, and flapped its wings in vain; then it was killed. Kunuk said it was excellent food, and dropped the tiny bird into the bag. He worked his way from ledge to ledge, from boulder to boulder, guided by the cries; and caught sixty-six of these creatures that day.

The Eskimos have harvested birds here for centuries. There was old birds' dung on the rocks, moss-covered stones, and luxuriant green grass between the boulders. A fox barked in the rock pile. Birds took to the air as we advanced, spread out their wings, and sailed toward the sea. They circled and came back, kept circling until we had gone. An Eskimo dog was sitting on a ledge; he too was catching birds.

The old Eskimos had a special way of catching auklets and puffins, we were told. They made a net of sinews, a couple of feet in diameter, and attached it to the end of a long pole. The first bird they caught in the net they used as a decoy. They tied it to the end of a long skin rope fastened through the bird's nostril with the aid of a baleen splinter. The bird was thus hung on the line alive and its fluttering attracted the curiosity of other birds, and as they came within reach of the net they were caught.

We climbed from one boulder to the other, traversing the mountain, heading for the summit at the extreme end of the cape. Below us the breakers thundered against the rocks, white froth foamed as the waves smashed against the shore. The air was alive with flapping wings, thousands of birds hovered between the mountain and the sea. They were sitting along the face of the mountain all the way up to the summit, packed so densely that they pushed each other off as more birds continued to land.

On our return to the village we passed near the old graveyard. From a distance we could see the gleaming wooden coffins in the rock pile. One of them was open, apparently hit by a stone during a landslide at some time. On the edge, resting against the rock, there was a cranium grinning at us, and in the box were the rest of a woman's bones, partly covered by moss. Here and there coffins had been shoved in among the stones. Women and children were placed farthest down at the foot of the mountain, Kunuk explained. Highest up on the slope were the coffins of the greatest hunters, with their implements and weapons.

It started to rain; the fog descended upon the village so thickly that we could barely see the ocean beyond it. Everything looked dreary, gray and wet; even the dogs were silent. From the mountain the village looked like a jumble of wooden, unpainted houses upon gray gravel, haphazardly placed here and there in irregular rows. They were built of frames covered with boards of sun-bleached wood. Gray skin boats rested on the platforms by the sea.

In the hallway of Kunuk's house there was a strong odor, judged by noses not yet accustomed to rotten blubber. The wet, slippery dirt floor was covered with oil and dog droppings. The family lived in a single room, damp and dark. Moisture dripped from the roof; cooking utensils and tin cans had been placed in the pools of water on the floor or hung up under the roof where the leakage was most pronounced. There was a bunk along the wall, and on it sat Kunuk's wife, who had come as a child from Siberia with her parents.

"My wife is sad when it rains," he said. "The house is in poor condition; I need new tarboard for the roof."

The house shook with every gust of wind, and it was drafty. The light went out and they fussed with the lamp. The stove was dead, but no one attended to it.

The rain came in showers; puddles of water formed between the houses. The dogs stood along the walls shivering, with their tails tucked between their legs. The grass swayed in the wind; the houses were gray and soaked in water, with rubbish stacked on the roofs. Now and then an Eskimo came out of one of the buildings, wading through the puddles sliding on the greasy doorsteps. A man appeared with a pot which he emptied into a hole in the ground; the pups were fighting to get to it.

Every time a child opened the door we could hear the roar of the sea, the hissing and rushing of waves and breakers pounding at the beach. The spray from the sea was carried by the wind like a drizzling rain. Sea gulls sailed quietly with lazy wing strokes over the breakers. Auklets scurried clumsily along over the sea.

We offered Kunuk a cigarette, which he accepted with

a delighted expression, "I tried hard to learn to smoke," he said, "now I am trying even harder to learn to quit."

While his wife started to prepare the birds he had brought home, he continued to chat. Like most Eskimos, he liked to talk once he got started, and he talked freely about everything. He spoke a simple English, with almost poetically constructed sentences and with a singing intonation.

He had been born on South Cape. For a while he herded reindeer at Savoonga, where he had the opportunity to go to school, though only for a couple of weeks altogether. He lived with his grandparents and several of his uncles and aunts. They ate on the floor around a single tray loaded with meat, drinking the broth of the boiled meat as a beverage. He could remember a period of starvation when he was a boy, when the storm lasted several months so that they were unable to go hunting. At the end they chewed the boiled skins of bearded seal. There were sick people in every house, lying on the floor coughing and unable to eat. His father was seriously ill, and they thought he was going to die.

One day he said to Kunuk that he wished he had some oba, a kind of sea food with a shell like a ball full of needles. It was generally known that one could always find lots of oba by the old camp site at Dapok on the north side of the island.

Kunuk harnessed his dogs, mapped out his course, and drove his team by the compass for about three hours through the storm to Dapok. When he arrived he found an old man named Timkaro seriously ill. Timkaro had once drifted away with the pack ice to Siberia when he was caught in a storm while hunting, and did not return to the island until several years later.

Now he found old Timkaro lying on his back covered by skins, with a log of driftwood under his head. He was almost motionless, as if he were dead, not even moving his head when he spoke. He asked Kunuk to go to Sevuokok to tell his relatives that he was sick; would they please come to see him.

Timkaro's wife was up and about, but she looked ill and was coughing. Their twelve-year-old son was active and appeared well. Kunuk asked Timkaro to stay put, and promised that as soon as the weather improved he would go to Sevuokok with his message. Then he gathered his oba, which the storm had washed up on the beach in large quantities, and returned to his father.

It was a terrible blizzard; the wind swept the dogs off their feet; time and time again he himself was nearly blown off the cliff. He had to go ahead to guide the dogs, and almost walked past his house in the gale.

Three days later the weather improved sufficiently so that he could drive to Sevuokok with the message to Timkaro's relatives. Before he got there, however, he met Tingmiak up on the mountain, who told him that they had already found Timkaro and his wife dead in the snow.

Old Timkaro had decided to journey to Sevuokok after all. It is customary among the Eskimos that if they are taken ill in the mountains or on the tundra they will try to get back to the village, come hell or high water, explained Kunuk. The old woman and the boy had carried Timkaro to the sled, and then headed for Sevuokok in the blizzard, but after a while the dogs refused to go on against the storm. The old man felt that his strength was fading, and he told them that if he were to die they were to place him in the snow and they themselves were to try to reach Sevuokok without him.

Timkaro died twenty miles from Sevuokok; they left him in the snow and drove on through the blizzard. Ten miles from the village the mother gave up, and the dogs were exhausted. It was the middle of the night and still blowing hard. The woman sat down in the snow and asked the boy to go on to get help.

At this point, Kunuk was visibly moved as he continued his story.

The boy set out, he said, but was reluctant to leave his mother behind, and turned back. Three times he set out, but returned each time. The third time he failed to find her in the blinding blizzard, so he kept on walking. Eventually, he had to sit down to rest; he leaned back and fell asleep. When he woke up, his left hand was frostbitten. He staggered on through the snow.

It so happened that one of the young men from Sevuokok had a trapper's cabin in the mountains and decided to go there to take care of his traps, in spite of the weather; so it was that he met the boy some six miles south of the village. As soon as they got back to Sevuokok, all those who had dog teams set out to search for the couple. The search went on throughout the night. Finally an Eskimo boy found the woman, sitting in the snow, leaning forward supporting her head in her arms. She might be alive, maybe she was too weak to shout, or perhaps she was dead, but according to Eskimo custom it was taboo for him to touch her; so he returned to the village. In the summer, when the snow had melted, somebody found the dead woman in the mountain again. They also found Timkaro where he had been left.

"This is the only case of an Eskimo freezing to death here on the island, as far as I know," said Kunuk, "and had it not been for the fact that they were sick to start with, it would never have happened." He went on to·say that occasionally an Eskimo suffers frostbite, like everyone else, on the face, on the nose and ears, and on the hands too, for that matter, but as a rule this is the result of an accident. They may go through the ice, or their clothes may be torn, but "he who is smart carries always a needle and some thread in the pocket, so that he may do some mending if need be," said Kunuk.

Then he told us of old Nasaga who was once caught in a terrific snowstorm on his way to Savoonga. He got lost and wandered around for two whole weeks. Once in a while he would sit down on the sled to sleep a couple of hours until he would start to shiver so violently that he woke up; then he would drive on for a while. In this manner he kept going in spite of the cold and the storm. He was eventually found near South Cape in good health and without any frostbite.

He had been wearing a pair of sealskin socks on his feet, and had plenty of dried grass in his sealskin mukluks. Next to the skin he had a pair of reindeer skin trousers with the fur side in, and on top of these a pair of sealskin trousers with the hair side out. He wore a parka of auklet skins with the feathers facing inward, and outside it another parka of bird skins with the feathers facing out. On top of it he had a windbreaker made of walrus intestines. On his hands he had two pairs of sealskin mittens. He had no sleeping bag.

We asked Kunuk how the feather parkas were made, and he explained that during the preparation of the raw bird skins they are turned inside out and dried; formerly they were then put into a large vessel filled with urine, where they remained several weeks until the fat turned white. Today soap and water are used instead. After soaking they are taken up and the fat scraped off the skins. Following this they are again dried, and finally rubbed until they become quite soft and pliable and are ready to be sewn together into parkas. Twenty-five cormorant skins are required for a single parka. The skins are so arranged that the feathers point downward in order that the snow will not stick to them. The bird-skin parkas are light and warm, but according to Kunuk they always retain a strong smell of the cormorant skins.

After a pause he went on with his own story. "Most of the people who lived at South Cape died of starvation," he said. "My family was among the last to leave. Some of them settled at Savoonga, others came with us to Sevuokok. I was only nineteen at that time."

Then he smiled with apparent pride. "I had to work two years for my wife," he said. "My father and my uncles gathered a lot of fur, mukluks, utensils and groceries which they bought at the store and presented it all to her mother. Then I moved into her parents' house and worked for them. I had to do as they told me; I hunted for them, and ate on their floor. At night we all undressed. The menfolk had nothing but a rag around their middle, the women some very short pants. We bedded down on reindeer skins laid on the floor with the hair facing up; and as bed covers we used sealskins with the hair side away from the body or bird skins with the feathers out. That is how we slept," he insisted.

During the night he would approach his fiancée. She was not at all unwilling, as might perhaps be expected, but at times he made so much noise that he awakened the rest of the family. "But, even so, no one said anything," he said with a laugh.

Sexual intercourse was such a natural thing among the Eskimos that it was regularly witnessed even by the children. It was hardly to be avoided, anyhow, the way they slept packed together side by side on the floor.

According to Eskimo tradition, an old widower was entitled to approach a young girl, Kunuk told us. If the girl's father gave his consent, he would receive gifts and allow the widower to work for his daughter, whether the girl wanted him or not. If she was against it, it was up to the man to persuade her to change her mind. He would, as a rule, wait until the girl had gone to sleep. If she resisted, he had to leave it at that and could only hope for better luck some other time. This might go on for some time, and if she finally gave in she had to accept him as her husband. So simple was their entire wedding ceremony then.

It was not at all unusual for the mother to side with a reluctant daughter and stay awake most of the night for her sake. However, if the suitor was an outstanding hunter and a valuable member of the father's boat crew, the father himself would be interested in protracting the wooing, because the longer it lasted the longer he could enjoy the man's service free of charge on his boat.

When the father decided that it was time to consider the matrimonial requirements accomplished, he would take his daughter, completely fitted out with an assortment of utensils and equipment, over to the house of his prospective son-in-law, and the two were by that act considered legally married. Divorce, Kunuk assured us, was rare.

The practice of buying a wife with presents still continues on the island; it occurred while we were at Sevuokok, but we never saw the Eskimos show any signs of affection in their daily life, by rubbing noses or by other acts of love.

Bigamy was common up to some years ago, and there were still old men on the island who had two wives. There was old Ujarak, for instance, whose two wives came from Siberia. The first one failed to get any children; she then selected a wife number two for her husband, and all went smoothly. "They say that some Eskimos in Siberia had as many as ten wives," said Kunuk, and appeared to be impressed.

When we asked if there was any jealousy, he said that this occurred mostly among the young people. "If a husband discovers that his wife has been unfaithful, he gets angry; he may beat her with a stick. If the wife finds out that her husband has had another woman, she attacks him with her nails; she may pull his hair and bite him. There are certain women who have a tendency to be unfaithful," he observed, "women who are not properly taken care of by their husbands in the first place, perhaps.

"In the olden days it was different, however. Fifteen years ago the swapping of wives was commonplace. Take, for instance, Talek and Inuk. Those two fellows agreed to go ahead and sleep with each other's wives. It happened that one of them even took the other man's wife along on his hunting trips. The reason for this was simply that they wanted children, especially sons, to take part in the hunting. A few years ago, two men who were childless swapped wives. One of the women became pregnant and gave birth to a child; the other one was unsuccessful. No one was supposed to know about the deal because the authorities do not favor such arrangements nowadays," he added.

"The boys may begin to get experience with the girls at the age of about thirteen," he continued. "They may find a suitable place in a meat cache, in a storm shed, or behind a hill. It does not matter where it is, as long as no one can see them. If they are caught in the act they may be punished, as a rule by a fine. The old men keep a keen eye on them, sitting by the window or standing at the corner; they do not miss very much, these old men. However, when the old men are asleep at night, there is a great deal of love-making going on among the youths."

Hair on the body other than on the head is sparse in the Eskimo. Pubic hair is often completely absent in the women, and there appears to be a direct relationship between racial purity and lack of pubic hair.

The beard starts to grow on boys about fourteen years of age. At the same time their voices begin to change. The girl's breasts start to grow during the thirteenth year, and menstruation starts at twelve to fourteen years of age. According to Kunuk, many Eskimo girls are mothers at the age of fourteen. If a girl became pregnant before she was married, the old women used to try to produce an abortion by applying pressure on the stomach.

The girls may be rather aggressive at times. Some of them are apparently proud of the fact that they have had an affair with a white man and would like it to be generally known. One night one of our technicians was awakened by the noise of someone moving about in the room. He was startled and sat up so suddenly that he almost bumped his head against a person standing by the bed.

"Who is it?"

"Pinega," replied a woman's voice from the darkness. It meant "I love you," but this the technician did not know at the time. He asked what she wanted.

"Love you, lie beside you and talk a little."

The technician could now see that she was standing there nude under her overcoat, and it was not too dark for him to see also that she was not very young. He asked her to get out before she awakened his colleague, and when she left, he could hear more girls giggling outside the door.

As we were sitting by the window listening to what Kunuk had to say we could see a man come out from the house next door to empty a pot outside the wall. He took a look out to sea and discovered that a supply vessel had anchored a couple of hundred yards off the shore. He dropped the pot and started to run; soon the entire village was rushing toward the beach.

Then the sailors came ashore and invaded this simplehearted society. A weasel stopped with a jerk outside the house of Nona, a mature Eskimo woman of considerable attraction. The sailor kept the weasel running while he dashed into the house. He had no sooner entered the door than a small flock of Eskimo women rushed out. They hung around the house until the boy came out bareheaded and climbed into the weasel. As he turned the corner, Nona appeared in the door waving the sailor's hat, while the women giggled among themselves.

"They know so much about each other, these women, that they cannot afford to carry tales," explained Kunuk, and smiled at his wife, who did not know any English.

A messenger came to report that Sila was sick. She was in bed and was coughing up blood. There were several cases of tuberculosis in her family, Kunuk said.

He accompanied us over to her house. We crawled through the dark hallway over seal blubber, tackle, and birds partly chewed by the dogs, and entered a small room. It was dark and there was an odor of stagnant air; we slipped and slid on the oily floor. A kettle of water was boiling on a blubber stove in one corner. The blubber lamp was lit, the seal oil flowing over its edge and trickling onto the floor. Various garments were hanging under the ceiling to dry, scraps of food were scattered around. Sila's father sat in a corner boiling whale blubber over a primus.

The patient was lying nude on the floor between two greasy comforters, thumbing through a book. I knelt down to listen to her chest and came to the conclusion that she was suffering from pulmonary tuberculosis, a common condition among these people.

The schoolteacher appeared to say that he was concerned about the Inuks' little daughter. She was only a year old and had been under the weather ever since early spring; she was weak and drowsy, and now she was running a fever. They had been keeping watch over the child around the clock.

We went out into the rain, walked past the schoolhouse and between the shacks, which had mounds of empty tin cans piled around them. The Eskimos gather these empty cans and pile them up around their walls to show that they can afford to buy food at the store. This is their form of snobbery, their way of keeping up with the Joneses, we were told.

Again we crawled through a narrow hall reeking of rancid blubber and sweaty fur garments, and went into a room half lit by a kerosene lamp. Half a dozen men were seated on the floor, their legs stretched out, their backs against the wall. They greeted us with grave, scared looks. In a bed in a corner lay the child on her back with half-opened eyes filled with pus; the breathing was shallow and rapid, the cheeks were glowing red from the fever, the forehead clammy; otherwise the skin was sallow, with a yellowish tint. On each side of her head they had placed a Bible with a picture of Christ between them. A baby's milk bottle with a rubber nipple was propped up against one of the Bibles.

The mother sat in front of the bed braiding the sinews of a whale. The child's uncle, dressed in long underwear, sat with his back against the table; he had been nursing the child during the night. The child's father was away at the fishing camp. The mother gave us a sad look. We knew that she had previously lost two babies the same way. She said she was glad that we could come, and gave us a piece of sinew as a token of gratitude.

We examined the child, who by now was lying with her head bent backward; her arms and legs were stiff and extended, her pupils failed to react to light, and there was evidence of increased intracranial pressure. She had meningitis. We knew that tuberculous meningitis was by no means rare in Sevuokok, and in this particular family all suffered from tuberculosis.

We did everything we possibly could do, and stayed with her the whole evening. She was unconscious and shivering faintly when we put out the light over her bed. Helpless, we went away, wishing there was something we could do for her. She would probably not live through the night.

The mother thanked us for our help and said that the child was all that she had left now. She had been so frightened before we came; now she felt safer, she said. This made us feel even worse, for we knew only too well that there was nothing more we could do.

The child awakened at midnight and cried once, then she slumbered on, never to wake again.

The day came with a bright sun in a clear sky. In the village life went on as usual. The old men stood on the gravel hills scanning the ocean, the children played, their clear voices ringing between the houses as they ran about. Bowlegged old women trotted along to share their fun, like all grandmothers. The mailman bustled in and out among the houses, dressed in his soldier's topcoat, peaked cap, and tuxedo trousers stuffed into high rubber boots. Dogs were barking and an old Eskimo was patiently painting the newly completed skin boat.

Down by the beach Waloonga was making his umiak ready to take his family to Savoonga. The men loaded the boat, while Waloonga's wife watched with apparent indifference. Twenty years ago it was she who had to row the boat; now they have an outboard motor, and no one but the skipper is allowed to tamper with it.

In Inuk's house, they were still waiting for the father of the child to come home. They had decided to wait until about three o'clock in the afternoon, when they would start to make the coffin. This is part of the funeral ceremony. In the afternoon, the child's relatives and the elders in the village gathered around the body to pray. They placed her body, wrapped in a woolly blanket, in a homemade coffin of wood; then the lid was nailed into place.

Up to now everyone had been silent, without tears, but now the little brother could not control himself any longer. He sobbed and coughed, for he too had tuberculosis.

Then they placed the coffin on a square piece of walrus skin, and six Eskimo men carried it out of the house. At this moment the child's fifteen-year-old sister arrived; she met them in the door and remained standing there weeping alone while they continued with the coffin across the tundra into the mountain.

13 NEW HORIZONS

The time passed. We completed our initial two years in Alaska and returned to Norway in 1952 to work up our results and "recharge our batteries" in the Department of Physiology of the University of Oslo. In 1954 we were back in Alaska; this time I served as Director of Research of the Arctic Aeromedical Laboratory and helped develop and expand this institution until we left the Arctic for good in 1957. During these years we continued our work among the Eskimo tribes and observed the gradual change in their diet, clothing and culture.

Air communication was improving and eventually we had access to the remotest corners of Alaska, along the coast and up along the rivers, where we previously had been unable to land. The Eskimos themselves became pilots who flew us from Kotzebue and Point Barrow to Wainwright, Point Lay and Point Hope. We felt safe with the Eskimos in the pilot's seat; this was not always the case with the white pilots, as, for instance, on that ill-fated autumn day we were to start from Point Lay. The heavy, clumsy, white pilot they called Furious Fritz arrived tired and bad-tempered in his Cessna, almost touching the rooftops in the fog, and landed in the mud by the lagoon. It was said that he occasionally went to sleep behind the stick while he was flying. The passengers had to poke him in the back to wake him up from time to time.

It had been freezing during the night and the ground was hard at daybreak, but by the time we were ready to leave the weather had turned mild with thaw and the mud stuck to the wheels of the plane. We piled into the double seat behind the pilot, with the sleeping bags and the packsacks in our laps. In front, beside the pilot, there was a pregnant Eskimo woman who was going to the hospital at Point Barrow to be delivered.

A strong wind was blowing in from the lagoon across the muddy runway. The pilot decided to make an attempt to take off across the rough tundra straight up against the wind. He kicked the mud off his boots and settled in his pilot's seat, then the Eskimos lifted the tail of the plane around so that he could go ahead. He put full power on the engine, but the wheels were stuck in the mud; the lumps whipped up by the propeller flew through the air and stuck to the leading edge of the wings. He barely came to a halt on the landbrink before plunging off the edge into the lagoon.

The Eskimos grabbed hold of the tail and turned us around once more. This time the pilot wanted to try the regular landing strip running along the lagoon. There was more room here, so it would probably be all right, he mumbled to himself, and said something to the effect that there was a dance scheduled at Point Barrow that night.

He lined up on a hillock at the end of the runway which was marked by flags on both sides along the beach. Then he "gave her the gun" and we started to slide. We slalomed in and out among the flags; the flying mud splashed against the wings and fuselage; the engine roared, but there was no lift under the wings. We were stuck behind all the baggage and could not see a thing.

Now he has to quit, we thought as we approached the end of

the runway, with one wheel in the air and the other still rolling along on the ground. For a moment it looked as if he was going to head out over the lagoon, but fortunately he changed his mind in the last minute, because otherwise we would all have drowned.

Suddenly, before we had enough speed to fly, he jerked the airplane into the air, but since we had reached the very end of the runway, he no longer had any choice. We jumped a ditch, the wheels once more hit the ground, and we continued through the new-fallen snow across the niggerheads of the tundra heading straight for the village, with one wheel in the air.

The Eskimos who had seen us off to the plane were by now on their way back to the village. They stopped to stare at us. Ahead to our right we caught a glimpse of a woman with a child standing beside a fuel drum; we were heading straight for them. They threw themselves flat on the ground; in the next moment we thundered over them. We heard a bang and felt a jerk under our seats, then we started to flounder through the air. The pilot cut off the ignition, the engine stopped, and we came in for a crash landing on the tundra.

There was a whaleboat ahead of us next to a radio mast supported by wire struts. Beyond it the schoolhouse blocked our route. We plunged straight through the whaleboat, sending pieces of wood flying in all directions. At the same time one of the wings, caught in the struts of the radio mast, pulled off, but at least this prevented us from somersaulting. We continued, dragging the wires along, slowed down as the wires tautened, and came to a halt.

The Eskimos rushed to open the door for us, but the door fell off its hinges by itself, and we fell out of the aircraft in a pile onto the ground. The Eskimos smiled as if they were enjoying the sight.

"Complete wreck," muttered the deflated Furious Fritz, and the pregnant woman walked quietly home as if nothing had happened.

However, it happened again three weeks later. We had been to Anaktuvuk Pass to draw blood samples for an experiment with radioactive iodine in connection with a study of endemic goiter; we were on our way home in the afternoon when the weather turned bad. The fog surrounded all the hills, it started to rain, and soon it was dusk. At the end, we found ourselves in a valley surrounded by fog on three sides, and before we could turn around to get out of this hole, the fog curtain had completely closed our retreat. Below us we could barely distinguish a road in the dusk and the light from a trapper's cabin in the wilderness.

"There is only one thing to do," said the pilot; "we have to land here on the road before it is dark. It should be all right, I landed here once six years ago."

He made a pass, circled the road once, and as we passed over the treetops it occurred to me that there was not much room for the wings between the trees. In six years the forest had closed in on the road.

The pilot had picked a spot beyond a bridge where a gravel pit by the roadside gave us more room. We came in over the bridge, but touched down too far along the road and missed the selected landing spot where there was more space between the trees. We soared along at sixty miles an hour down the road, with the wingtips touching the branches; then the left wing started to hit the tree trunks. There was not enough room after all.

"God damn it," said the pilot with emphasis on every word. He had no sooner said this than the wing was caught in a spruce tree. Before we knew it we were heading for the woods as the plane made a ground loop and came to a sudden halt with one of the wheels in a ditch.

We climbed down and stretched out the radio antenna along the road, and called Fairbanks on the radio to order a taxi. At this point a carful of men who had been out hunting moose came by. They had had a few drinks and apparently thought they were having hallucinations when they saw the aircraft in the ditch. They drove us to our laboratory with our blood samples, and we completed our experiments according to schedule.

It happened to be our last experiment; with it our Eskimo studies were completed.

Our investigations had convinced us that the Eskimo's ability to get along in the arctic environment does not depend on built-in endowments or racial peculiarities or on real physiological acclimatization. It is simply due to the fact that the Eskimo has completely adjusted himself to the environment. From childhood he is brought up in the art of arctic living. His mind is at ease, for he knows of no better life beyond the bulwarks of the frozen seas. When he is old enough to face the elements alone he is fully versed in the technique of survival in the Arctic, and knows how to take care of himself and his family. From childhood he has developed a liking for a diet of meat which stimulates metabolism to greater heat production. His simple but practical garments of fur offer a far better insulation against the cold than anything we can manufacture, and he is smart enough to avoid the extreme cold by staying indoors in foul weather. In the final analysis his ability to withstand the cold depends to a large extent on his ability to avoid it effectively. If he has to be exposed to severe cold he possesses a degree of physical fitness developed through a lifetime of vigorous physical exercise, which allows him to keep going almost indefinitely at a steady pace, just fast enough to maintain his body heat without causing exhaustion.

Here is a people with a culture that dates back some twenty-five hundred years. They represent a homogeneous ethnic group that has developed a high degree of specialization and has survived by virtue of its ingenious simplicity.

There are some 15,000 Eskimos in Alaska today, and the vital statistics show a steady increase. Births are increasing, and improved hygiene and care enables more babies to survive the first years of life. Of those who survive the period of childhood many live to an old age.

Does this mean that the number of full-blooded Eskimos is increasing or does it merely mean an increase in the number of Eskimos mixed with white blood? If the latter is the case, is it possible that the Eskimo blood is being diluted and that the Eskimo race is about to become lost in the white race?

It is true that many Eskimos move to the towns and are lost to the Eskimo society. It is also true that many of the Eskimo women have children conceived by white men, but this mixing of blood takes place only on the female side; one rarely sees an Eskimo marry and have children with a white woman.

In the Eskimo settlements these half-breeds have the opportunity to marry full-blooded Eskimos, and their offspring are, in such cases, more Eskimo than white. There is also a tendency for Eskimos who had previously moved to the towns to return to their native villages to marry. This to some extent counteracts the dilution of the blood. It is therefore possible that the mixing with the white race will take place far more slowly than is generally believed.

The Eskimos have always lived under humble unhygienic conditions. This, however, may not have been a serious handicap earlier when they were isolated from the microbes which our civilization has brought along with it, microbes to which the Eskimos have little or no immunity. The result has been much destruction of human life. And to make things worse, the whites are partly responsible for settling the Eskimo tribes in villages around the churches and the schools, while before they were largely nomads on endless migration, following the game. Our civilization caused them to give up their simple, inexpensive sod houses which they could readily abandon without suffering any serious loss, and which required very little fuel. It caused them to abandon their skin tents which they sun-sterilized, so to speak, once every year. These were replaced with permanent, expensive, wooden houses where the dirt accumulates from year to year, and which require a great deal of fuel for heating—and fuel is a critical item along the arctic coast.

We have given the Eskimo our foodstuffs, and of these he has primarily selected the least valuable items. The result is that his diet today is often far inferior to that of his ancestors. This perhaps contributes further to his lowered resistance to disease, not to mention the fact that it has brought about a shocking decay of his teeth. The primitive Eskimos had perfect teeth, but the dental condition in those Eskimos who subsist on our white man's diet is incredible.

We have given the Eskimos our white man's clothing to replace his own, which was superior to ours. This the Eskimo himself realizes, but it so happens that he prefers to look like a white.

We have taken the Eskimo youngster away from the old men who would have taught him how to live off the land, to provide for his family from the harvests of the sea and land, by hunting and fishing, and placed him on the school bench to learn our language and the multiplication tables. We have taken away from him the basis for his natural livelihood without giving him in return a real basis for competing on an equal footing with the whites.

And during this process we have failed to inculcate in him the hygienic principles required to combat infections and communicable diseases. All available evidence suggests that the Eskimos were healthy people with great vitality before the whites came. The whites brought with them, in the wake of their whalers, epidemics of smallpox, measles, diphtheria, influenza and tuberculosis. This resulted in a decline in the population to about half. Even today the infant mortality rate among the Eskimos is twice as high as that of the United States. Tuberculosis causes thirty times more deaths among the

Eskimos than among the whites in America.

These are the conditions under which this Stone Age people is plunging into our civilization, staggering on toward new horizons.

It is notably in the larger cities, such as Fairbanks, that the Eskimos encounter the new era with all its implications and consequences. It is in the Super Bar on Main Street that all the Eskimos in town get together. The bar is a run-down shack with stalls around the walls and red-painted light bulbs which hardly shed any light at all. A couple of whisky bottles and a few rows of beer glasses on the counter are all that the bar has to offer. This is their meeting place. Here they come at all times of the day or night, both those who make good wages and those who have nothing at all. Some of them may order a drink; others just sit there without touching the liquor. This is where they meet their friends and acquaintances; this is where they satisfy their desire for news, pick up gossip from their village on the coast; and here they may even beat their drums and dance on occasion.

And here all kinds of whites may drop in, obese ones with bags around their eyes, and noses shining like beacons, skinny ones with hands shaking from hang-overs. Some are intoxicated and carry scars from previous fights, others are sober veterans of the wilderness.

It was in this Super Bar that we found Akiviak's son. He was sitting in a stall by himself; he had parked his car in the street outside; it was brand-new and expensive, fully equipped with a radio and all kinds of gadgets. He was working as a carpenter on a construction project; he worked overtime seven days a week and made some $5 an hour. He was a bachelor and felt lonely in Fairbanks. His sister had lived there awhile, but now she was married and had moved to the States to live. He had not heard from the rest of the family for months. He lived in a room in a house across the river, ate out or fixed his own meals, went to the movies every time they put on a new picture; otherwise he whiled away his spare time here at the bar.

We happened to meet him again on the plane going to Kaktovik one day in the spring. He was on his way to the coast to work as a carpenter at a construction site. And while we were sitting on the plane talking to a representative of a welfare organization who was bound for Kaktovik to examine the need for unemployment compensation among the Eskimos there, the copilot came out of the pilot's cabin to stretch his legs. It was he who had been the teacher at Kaktovik the first time we were there. He showed us a snapshot of the baby we had delivered; by now she had grown into an attractive little girl. She was living with his parents in New York City; he and his wife were divorced.

"There are fewer and fewer people in the village and more and more of them are resting upon the hill at Kaktovik. The rest of them are scattered everywhere." Thus he summed up the situation at Kaktovik.

There was a brilliant sunshine over the pack ice, so bright that it was painful to the eyes, when we landed. Much of the snow had already gone. Here and there the tundra showed through, as did the remnants of the rubbish which had been buried by the winter blizzards. There was black earth with moss and heather on the hilltops where the sun beat most strongly. An occasional snow bunting swept across the sooty snow, otherwise no life stirred on the tundra.

Large permanent buildings were scattered around the airfield where before there had been nothing but shacks, and in the village there were only seventeen Eskimos left. All the old people were gone and many of the youngsters had left; some of them had moved west to the coast where they made $100 a week; others had gone east to Herschel Island.

It was quiet among the houses in the village, the dogs were gone; there were no children playing around the igloos any more. A snow bunting sat on a pole tilting its head, its broad white breast glittering in the evening sun.

We went into Akiviak's old home. The house was empty and there was a padlock on the inner door. We went from house to house. Finally we came upon one where there were people. A woman we remembered was sitting with a group of children around a homemade table. The oldest children were drawing pictures, the youngest were playing with building blocks. A baby was asleep in the bed. The floor was scrubbed and spotlessly white, cups and pots were neatly stacked away, the walls were freshly painted, and curtains framed the window.

The woman's hair was braided and put up at the back, her skin looked clean and healthy, her cheeks were rosy. Apparently she had recognized us as we entered, for she smiled faintly as she ran her fingers through the hair of the little girl who had taken refuge in her lap when we came in, and said something about its being a long time since Akiviak died.

The young Akiviak was up on the hill by the graveyard on the tundra. From there he could see the airfield and the hangars around it, the village with the houses down the landbrink toward the sea, and the pack ice moving with the current beyond.

For the Eskimos there is hardly any future, in more senses than one. They live today and do not worry about tomorrow.

We speak of the Eskimo problem as if it were only one single problem common to all Eskimos. The fact is that every village and every individual Eskimo in every single family has to be considered separately. Economically, socially, culturally and with respect to education, a solution has to be found for each individual, according to his abilities, aspirations, motivation and character.

The Eskimos consider themselves different from white people. Only after we had been able to show them that we could live like one of them, drive our dogs alone, hunt the caribou independently, and take care of ourselves on the tundra and out on the ice did they consider us real human beings. And still it is difficult for us to get close to the Eskimos; it takes time to learn to understand them. Even the language is a barrier; they use "yes" when we use "no" to answer a negative question. If we say to an Eskimo whose name is Iyakitan, "You are not Slwooko by any chance?" he will answer "yes," meaning to say that it is correct that he is not Slwooko. That is how difficult it may be. One may ask the same question in three or four different ways and receive a different answer each time; and to top it off, the Eskimos dislike to be disagreeable. If one asks them to do something which they do not like to do, they will say yes and go and hide rather than risk becoming involved in a quarrel. By nature they are friendly and would like to give you the answer they think you want to hear. If you ask them what they had for breakfast, they may say "bacon and eggs," although you know for certain that they have seen neither bacon nor eggs for months. Without patience and understanding one gets nowhere with the Eskimo.

People fuss and write sad stories about those poor natives who once lived in peace and complete harmony until the white man arrived. The truth is that the Eskimos were not always so peaceful; they too fought and waged wars. Nor did they always enjoy peace and harmony within their own tribes; their own angakoks saw to that. Their minds were filled with the fear of evil spirits and taboos, superstition and idolatry, fear of the supernatural, fear of the elements. This of course is true of most primitive people anywhere, but there is a new kind of fear that we whites have introduced among the Eskimos—the fear of death.

In the original Eskimo society women were respected more than they are now and were sometimes included in the council of Eskimo leaders. However, even today one of the members of the village council at Wainwright is a woman.

Some tribes had strict rules about how women were to behave. The wife was not supposed to speak when there were men present. She was to take care of her man's clothes and fit him out for hunting trips. She was to serve food to the men and children first; she herself could eat later. The wife played an essential role in the daily life, however, and the rest of the family were directly dependent on her. Even today there is, as a rule, a definite separation between the duties of the man and the woman in the family. The man brings the game as far as the shore; there the wife takes over. But, as in our society, the man now does more to help the woman in the house than he used to.

However, when it comes to making decisions, it is the Eskimo man who wears the pants. And no major decision is made without lengthy discussions and deliberations. If several of them are contemplating making a hunting trip together, for instance, they may debate the matter for days on end, until there is unanimous agreement. Only one person speaks at a time, the rest of them listen tentatively until he has finished, then the next one has his say, and so they may carry on for hours, like the ancient Greeks at the time of Plato.

They always avoid violence and hardly ever inflict bodily harm on each other. From childhood they are taught not to lose their tempers. Maybe they achieve some sort of outlet in their easy amusement at other people's misfortunes.

We have to admit that by our standards the Eskimos' sexual morals are loose. But this may be because the sex life does not mean so much to them, it is not so involved with the emotions. Also, though no doubt the desire is present in both sexes, it is the woman who does the choosing and rejecting. The man is always out for what he can get, but the woman will accept only someone she likes.

At one time it was the custom for an Eskimo to lend out his wife, but this no longer happens. In the past, in Sevuokok, the men maintained a special relationship in this respect, which required the exchange of wives. This relationship was inheritable and was handed down from father to son like an unwritten law.

Their customs in bringing up children vary from strictness to complete absence of discipline. In some places they are extremely tolerant; the children are allowed to yell and to kick their parents, who merely give in and let them have their way, without any attempt at punishment. In other places the children hardly dare to make a noise; when they play indoors they have to stay in one corner; when they are disobedient they have to go to bed.

In our civilized society the children are allowed to play their way through school until they reach college age, when the need for hard work suddenly becomes apparent. We spend a lifetime preparing for a profession and become wise far too late in life. At the age of fifty a man is no longer in demand; at sixty-five he is usually forced to quit and thus withdraw his wealth of knowledge and his lifetime of experience, regardless of his fitness for physical and intellectual work.

In the old Eskimo society it was otherwise. The men continued to grow in usefulness and importance to the group as they aged; they grew in prestige, influence and economic importance. The old men were the best hunters; they were the first to spy the game because they rose early and were farsighted, and they knew best how to get it. Because of their wisdom and knowledge of the ice, the tundra, and the habits of the game animals they were respected by the young, who asked their advice and accepted their guidance and their decisions. Their word was law; they were the leaders who were necessary to the settlement and who were wanted and respected. Thus they continued to be useful members of the tribe until they themselves began to feel that they were getting old; then they rapidly withered away.

Now, however, respect for the older people is declining. It is especially noticeable that the young boys who have received a smattering of education show little respect for the aged. They think they know it all; nevertheless, when it comes to hunting and trapping they still come to the old men for advice, because when it really comes down to it the old men do know their business.

In earlier times they used to take the boys at the age of eight along on their hunting trips. I remember a boy at Wainwright who had to row in the umiak with the rest of the crew all day long without food. He kept on rowing until he fell asleep at the oar, but the father merely woke him up and told him to keep on rowing until they got home. The old men paid a great deal of attention to the boys, showed them where in the boat they could step, and how to walk on the ice, so that by the time they came of age they were seasoned hunters. And it was a man's personal ability in trapping and hunting as well as in leadership that created the respect. I remember the poor old man named Ikaq who walked about in filthy rags but was never laughed at, because he was a great hunter. The wealthy Kegak, on the other hand, hungered for prestige and wanted to be called Omalik, which stands for skipper, feeling that he warranted such an honor; the rest of the Eskimos, however, only laughed at him and thought it was funny when his house burned down.

This Ikaq called himself a Christian and went to church regularly, but he maintained his old superstitions in addition. He always said a prayer before the hunt, more or less in accordance with the old ritual, and he always said grace, even if it was only coffee he was about to receive. They all had in any case a natural respect for the food, which had some connection with an old taboo.

Christianity has confused the Eskimos. Now, for instance, they cannot hunt either Saturdays or Sundays in some of the villages, which does not make good sense to them. Fifteen years ago there were three semi-Christian families in Sevuokok; the rest of the population were heathens, from the missionaries' point of view. Today they are all Christian on paper, but few of them know what they really believe in. True enough, they go to church on Sunday, and some of them even carry two Bibles under their arms. But back in their own homes they believe in what they please, in stones which may bring them wind from the north and open water. And the faith of these people is strong, so strong in fact that they may be willing to die for it if need be.

Those who are responsible for the welfare of the Eskimos are greatly concerned. They provide free higher education for the gifted ones, and hope for the best. But many of those who are educated elect to return to their village, where they continue to hunt as before, without making use of their education. Others are trained as teachers with the idea that they will return to the village to teach the rest of the Eskimos, but many of those teachers remain in the towns and fail to go back.

In the evaluation of all this one has to keep in mind that we, as members of one culture, cannot judge the values and concepts, such as happiness, for example, of the members of another culture. One year a wealthy businessman from Chicago came as a tourist to Wainwright. He observed that the Eskimos lived in sod-covered igloos and had neither radios nor automobiles. He felt so sorry for these "unhappy" people that he sent them both. The automobile is still parked there on the tundra, and the Eskimos are not any happier for it.

Happiness has little to do with material values, at any rate not in the Eskimo society. We knew a splendid fellow from Point Hope who moved to Fairbanks and became a carpenter. Now he makes $10,000 a year and has never been so unhappy in all his life. In Point Hope he was respected and had friends, he was a leader and was in on everything. He lived happily with his wife and his son. In Fairbanks, on the other hand, he is

an outsider. He has lost contact with his own race because he
no longer can be satisfied with their humble conditions. He has
received too much education for that. But he does not have
much in common with the whites either; among them too he is
a misfit, and because contact with his fellow man is essential for
the well-being of an Eskimo he is miserable. He owns a car,
but he has nowhere to go. His wife has taken to the bottle, she
is no good any more, and he has nothing but trouble with his
son, who has run away from the school and is living on the
streets.

But there are others who have adjusted themselves well to
civilization and to life in the towns, where they can satisfy the
material needs they have learned to desire. Those who have
found their place among the whites hold their own. All cultures
have undergone the same transition. Our ancestors survived it.
It does not help anybody to say that this development is harmful to the Eskimos, that they ought to be isolated and made to
live as their forefathers did. We cannot continue to regard them
as museum pieces forever; they are far too alive for that.

The Eskimos are closely tied to their villages; they are always interested in what is going on there. This is the first thing
they ask about when they meet someone they know from home.
A couple of days away from home and they are homesick. They
are fond of their country, they like to hunt, they enjoy the life
in the villages and the freedom there, and, if one should venture
to predict their future, one may perhaps say that many of the
Eskimos would prefer to remain where they are, because they
are satisfied there. Others are bound to leave, of course, but of
these there will always be some who will return to the village to
stay there for the rest of their lives. In the long run, it will probably be with the Eskimos as with the yellow race in America;
they have become part of the society, but prefer to live by
themselves.

The aim must be to prepare the Eskimos gradually to tolerate our civilization, and the preparation has to start with pro-phylaxis. We must give them a real understanding of the basic principles of hygiene. As it now is, they know, for instance, that they are supposed to wash their hands when they eat, and so they eat first and wash their hands afterward, satisfied that they have washed as the teacher told them. How were they to understand that they were to wash their hands before touching the food? We must help them to develop sanitary conditions, a proper diet, medical and hospital care. We must help them to preserve their health. They themselves are capable of furnishing their own happiness. We have to create a healthy, stable economic basis for their existence first, and then little by little give them the rest of our cultural values, as they become ready for them: language, literature, art, higher education. But in this process we should be extremely careful not to take away from them the tradition of their ancestors, the noble aspects of their culture, their pride in themselves as a people, and their desire to maintain their self-identity. If their own language is lost, the myths, the legends, the storytelling will be lost with it. Unless we stimulate their interest, the Eskimo art, the Stone Age crafts and skills will vanish forever with the old men.

It does not do any good to take the young boy, who should be taught to become a hunter, away from his natural teaching master, the father, and place him on the school bench and teach him English, for with the small amount of English he learns he does not get very far in his competition with the whites. In doing this, all we have achieved is to render him dependent and unable to make his living as a hunter, to live off the land. We cannot pull from under the Eskimos the very basis of their existence without giving them a new foundation to stand on.

And still, when all is said and done, maybe these people will survive us and live to water the flowers on our graves. In any case, the one who is the least worried about the future is the Eskimo himself, as he continues to smile as his forefathers have smiled before him, and says in his own simple way that all is well—Ajungilak!

A GUIDE TO THE LINE DRAWINGS

TITLE PAGE: Blubber lamps (iperalik) are shallow vessels of pottery or stone used by the Eskimos to cook food and to heat and light their dwellings. The vessel is filled with blubber oil which is burned with the aid of a wick made of dried moss or similar material. The flame is regulated by varying the size of the wick.

PAGE 1: Eskimo ceremonial mask (kinapak) carved from whalebone. The lower lip in this particular mask has two ivory labrets. Such labrets made of walrus-tusk ivory or jade were worn by many primitive tribes as personal ornaments. The labrets were fitted into holes pierced through the lip.

PAGE 15: Eskimo drum (krilaūt) made from stomach skin of the walrus stretched over a wooden frame. The edges of the drumskin are tied to the frame with sinew.

PAGE 40: Model of sailing vessel made by the Wainwright Eskimos from baleen.

PAGE 54: Jade ax (ulimaut) fashioned from a piece of sharp Alaskan jade fixed to a shaft made from caribou antlers.

PAGE 61: Seal harpoon (nauligak) consisting of a shaft made of narval tusk, a foreshaft of bone and a loose head of ivory with an inset cutting point. The detachable harpoon head is fixed to a long skin line, the other end of the line being tied to a float or held in the hunter's hand. As the harpoon head is thrust deep into the animal, the head is dislodged from the shaft. When tension is applied to the line, the harpoon head turns sideways and is firmly anchored in the body of the animal. The rear end of the harpoon shaft is pointed and is used as an ice pick.

PAGE 78:   Harpoon head (sakku) from St. Lawrence Island.

PAGE 89:   Wooden meat bowl or tray (kaiyootak) used for the family meal.

PAGE 97:   Snow goggles worn to protect the eyes from direct sunshine and from bright glare reflected by the snow surface, as a preventive measure against snow blindness. These goggles are made from caribou hoofs in which thin perforations are made for eye slits. They are held in place by straps of caribou skin.

PAGE 107:   The wolf scarer is a piece of baleen attached to a string of sinew. When it is whirled over one's head, the screaming, whining sound thus produced scares the wolves away.

PAGE 125:   A kayak, used for hunting sea mammals. It consists of a light wooden frame covered with skin. It is so light that it can easily be carried by a single man.

PAGE 135:   Bird rookery carved out of a walrus tusk by an Eskimo.

PAGE 165:   The ursuk, a bony structure which supports the male sex organ of the walrus. The length of this particular specimen is eighteen inches. These bones frequently show signs of healed fractures.

PAGE 184:   An Eskimo "jo-jo," two skin-covered balls connected with a braided sinew line. By jiggling the line up and down, the two balls are made to swing in a circular fashion in opposite directions without colliding. It is a favorite diversion of the St. Lawrence Island Eskimos, who play the game with great skill.

INDEX

Dr. Kaare Rodahl was born in Brönnöysund, Norway, near the Arctic Circle, and has always been concerned with the North. A graduate and former assistant professor of Oslo University's School of Medicine, he is not only an authority on arctic medicine and physiology, but a veteran of numerous scientific polar expeditions. These have taken him through most of the arctic regions from Spitsbergen in the east to the Bering Strait in the west. Dr. Rodahl has been fascinated by the Eskimos ever since he first encountered them in Greenland in 1939, and much of his work since then has been related to the Eskimo and his world.

During the Second World War he made 31 descents as a member of the Royal Norwegian Parachute Company. Later, at the invitation of the U.S.A.F., he became Director of Research at the Arctic Aeromedical Laboratory in Alaska. In 1952 he helped to plan and took part in the U.S. Air Force Ice Island Project which set up a scientific drift station (still in operation) on the famous ice island, T-3. This adventure he described brilliantly in his book *North*.

More recently he took part in an expedition to the Antarctic to establish a physiological research program at Little America.

Since 1957 Dr. Rodahl has been Director of Research at the Lankenau Hospital in Philadelphia. The author of several books and numerous magazine articles and scientific publications, he is also Chairman of the Panel on Biology and Medicine of the Committee on Polar Research of the National Academy of Sciences and an honorary member of the Staff and Faculty of the U.S. Army Command and General Staff College, Fort Leavenworth, Kansas.

He is married and the father of two children, Anton, 11, and Kari, 10.

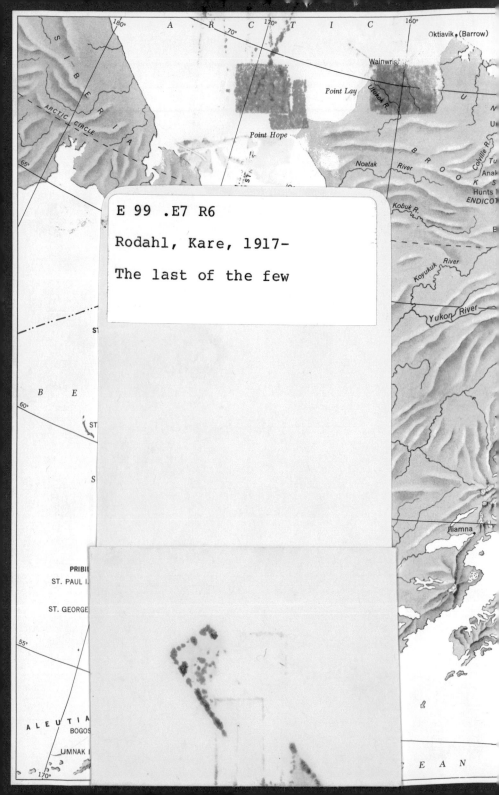